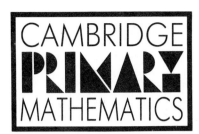

CAMBRIDGE PRIMARY MATHEMATICS

Module 4

Teacher's resource book

Roy Edwards, Mary Edwards
and Alan Ward

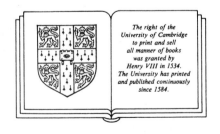

The right of the
University of Cambridge
to print and sell
all manner of books
was granted by
Henry VIII in 1534.
The University has printed
and published continuously
since 1584.

Cambridge University Press

Cambridge

New York   Port Chester   Melbourne   Sydney

Published by the Press Syndicate of the University of Cambridge
The Pitt Building, Trumpington Street, Cambridge CB2 1RP
32 East 57th Street, New York NY 10022, USA
10 Stamford Road, Oakleigh, Melbourne 3166, Australia

First published 1989

Printed in Great Britain by Scotprint, Musselburgh

British Library cataloguing in publication data

Cambridge primary mathematics
  Module 4
  Teachers resource book
  1. Mathematics – For schools
  I. Edwards, Roy   II. Edwards, Mary
  III. Ward, Alan
  510

  ISBN 0 521 35826 4

The authors and publishers would like to thank the many schools and
individuals who have commented on draft material for this course. In
particular, they would like to thank Ronalyn Hargreaves (Hyndburn Ethnic
Minority Support Service), John Hyland, Norma Pearce and Anita Straker,
who wrote the chapter on 'Using the computer'.

DP

CONTENTS

Mathematical content of chapters in Module 4

		Block 1		Block 2		Block 3
Number (mainly addition)	1	Number bonds to 20 Commutative property Place value of TU Addition of TU without exchanging	6	Addition of TU with exchanging Place value of HTU	11	Addition of HTU with exchanging from units Number patterns and magic squares
Number (mainly subtraction)	2	Number bonds to 20 Difference between two numbers Place value of TU Subtraction of TU without exchanging	7	Subtraction of TU with decomposition Place value of HTU	12	Subtraction of HTU with decomposition from tens Number patterns
Shape	1	Properties of the square, rectangle, circle, triangle, hexagon and pentagon	2	Properties of the cube, cuboid, cylinder, pyramid, cone, triangular prism and sphere	3	Bilateral or reflective symmetry Line of symmetry
Number (mainly multipli- cation)	3	Multiplication as repeated addition Commutative property Multiplication patterns for 2, 5, 10	8	Multiplication patterns for 3, 4, 5 Commutative property	13	Recording multiplication Linking addition and multiplication
					14	Multiplying 2 digits by a single digit (answers in TU only)
Area	1	Covering surfaces	2	Measuring area by counting squares	3	Measuring area by counting whole and half squares
Number (mainly division)	4	Sharing and grouping Link between multiplication and division Division by 2, 3, 4, 5	9	Division as repeated subtraction Division by 2, 3, 4, 5		
Data	1	Tallying and collecting data Block graphs (1:1 scale) Interpretation	2	Finding positions on grids	3	Block graphs (1:2 scale) Constructing and interpreting
Money	1	Coins to £1 Making up amounts Changing to coins of equal value	2	Bills and change	3	Notation for pounds and pence Addition and subtraction
Number (fractions)	5	Halves and quarters	10	Equivalence of ½, ¼	15	Introducing ¾ Finding ½, ¼, ¾ of shapes and quantities
Length	1	Measuring with digits, spans, cubits and strides Estimating	2	Measuring in centimetres Estimating	3	Addition and subtraction of cm Use of the metre
Weight	1	Balancing using non-standard weights Estimating	2	Weighing and balancing using gram weights	3	Introducing the kg, ½kg
Volume & Capacity	1	Filling and pouring activities using non-standard units Cube as a unit of volume	2	Use of litre, ½ litre		
Time	1	Days of the week Months of the year	2	o'clock, half past, quarter past Digital o'clock times	3	Introducing quarter to Minutes in 1 hour, ½ hour, ¼ hour Digital times for half past, quarter past
Angles	1	Left and right turns	2	½, ¼ turns	3	Introducing the right-angle Clockwise and anti-clockwise

INTRODUCTION

Aims

Cambridge Primary Mathematics is designed for 4–11 year old children. It takes into account current thinking in mathematical education and in particular it provides opportunities for:

- exposition
- discussion
- practical work
- consolidation and practice
- problem-solving
- investigational work

It is also designed to make mathematics relevant for the children and there is considerable emphasis on presenting the mathematics in real situations. Calculator work is incorporated throughout at the discretion of the teacher and ideas are given for using the computer. The materials are for children of all abilities and particular thought has been given to those with special educational needs.

Cambridge Primary Mathematics provides you with a sound foundation for all your mathematics teaching. It is *not* trying to take the place of a teacher, but rather acknowledge your professionalism. All the materials that make up Cambridge Primary Mathematics are giving you, the teacher, a core of valuable resources, so you can teach mathematics in whatever way suits you best. Cambridge Primary Mathematics can be used in its entirety and does not need additional material in order to provide a thorough mathematics curriculum. However, you may prefer to teach using a variety of materials and Cambridge Primary Mathematics will give you a rich source of teaching ideas which you can supplement.

The materials

Each topic can be introduced to a class or group with activities and discussion. Ideas for these are given in the teaching notes. The children can then try the relevant chapter in the pupils' book.

Pupils' books

Each chapter in the pupils' books has its concepts developed in three stages.

Section A is intended for all children and care has been taken to make it easily accessible. It consolidates the introduction, discussion and

Module	For teachers	Pupils' core materials	Reinforcement and enrichment				Assessment
1 4–5 yrs	Module 1 Teacher's resource pack	Module 1 Workbooks	Module 1 Games pack Module 1 Extra cut-up cards and rules Module 1 Rhymes pack				
2 5–6 yrs	Module 2 Teacher's resource pack	Module 2 Workcards	Module 2 Games pack Module 2 Extra cut-up cards and rules				
3 6–7 yrs	Module 3 Teacher's resource	Module 3 Workcards	Module 3 Games pack Module 3 Extra cut-up cards and rules				pack
4 7–8 yrs	Module 4 Teacher's resource book	Module 4 Book 1 Module 4 Answer book Module 4 Book 2	Module 4 Skill support activities	Module 4 Games pack Module 4 Puzzle pack Module 4 and Module 5 Project booklets	S O F T W A R E		Module 4 Assessment pack
5 8–9 yrs	Module 5 Teacher's resource book	Module 5 Book 1 Module 5 Answer book Module 5 Book 2	Module 5 Skill support activities	Module 5 Games pack Module 5 Puzzle pack			Module 5 Assessment pack
6 9–10 yrs	Module 6 Teacher's resource book	Module 6 Book 1 Module 6 Answer book Module 6 Book 2	Module 6 Skill support activities	Module 6 Games pack Module 6 Puzzle pack Module 6 and Module 7 Project booklets			Module 6 Assessment pack
7 10–11 yrs	Module 7 Teacher's resource book	Module 7 Book 1 Module 7 Answer book Module 7 Book 2	Module 7 Skill support activities	Module 7 Games pack Module 7 Puzzle pack			Module 7 Assessment pack

practical work provided by the teacher and finishes with a problem or investigation. Children who need further reinforcement can be given work from the skill support masters.

Section B is suitable for the majority of children and covers the same concepts in more breadth, and again includes an investigation.

Section C, which includes a further investigation, can be used as extension work.

The work in these sections is usually based on a theme of interest to children (e.g. the school trip, animals, etc.) in order to give the material more cohesion and to make it relevant to the environment.

This structure ensures that all children can follow a basic course of mathematics, covering all the concepts at whatever stage is appropriate to them. Organisationally this allows the teacher to teach the children as a class or in groups, as all sections cover the same topics but at increasing breadth. Children who complete only section A will not be left behind in the progression. The A, B, C format will provide for problem-solving and investigational skills to be developed across all areas of the mathematics curriculum by all children.

Logos

Throughout the pupils' books, certain logos are used to show children the items they will need or which would be particularly helpful.

shows that squared paper is needed.

 means a clock face stamp would be useful.

 tells children they can time themselves.

 indicates that a calculator would be useful.

 shows that glue is required.

The logos are used partly to reduce the language in instructions and partly to give children visual clues for items they need.

Coloured text

Two colours of text are used in the pupils' books in order to help the children. Black text is used for instructions and information. Blue text shows the parts the children will need to record in their books.

Answer books

The answer books contain reduced facsimiles of the pages in the pupils' books. The answers are superimposed.

Games packs

There is a games pack for each module. The games are linked to the mathematical content of the course and are intended to consolidate children's skills and also to encourage children in logical thinking and development of strategies.

Puzzle packs

There is a puzzle pack for each module. These packs provide extra extension material and additional interest.

Skill support activities

The packs provide extra work for those children who need it. One set consolidates the basic concepts, and another set develops the concepts still further for the more able.

Project booklets

These are written for use by pupils and provide opportunities for project work and the linking of mathematics with the environment and with other areas of the curriculum.

Software

The software is intended to develop problem-solving skills. It is not linked to any particular chapters.

Organisation and management

The materials needed are readily available, but to help you further there is a complete list of all equipment required at the end of this book. Materials can be collected, boxed and labelled so that they are easily accessible to the children. Picture labels will help those with reading problems.

Cambridge Primary Mathematics is not intended as a scheme for children to work at individually, but instead to give you control over how the mathematics is taught. The following ideas have been suggested by teachers who used the early materials.

- Introduce each topic using your own ideas plus the information in the teacher's notes.
- Let children develop the concepts at their own levels using the A, B, C structure and the skill support masters.
- Some of the investigations are particularly suitable for work and discussion in a large group or whole class.
- Overcome a shortage of equipment, like balance scales, by organising groups to work at several different activities.
- Use the games and puzzles to reinforce particular teaching points or skills as part of the normal mathematics lesson.
- Look for the calculator games in the teacher's notes.

Cambridge Primary Mathematics gives you the space to include your own ideas and to develop concepts as part of the whole curriculum.

Using the teacher's resource book

There is a section in the teacher's book for each chapter of the pupils' material. The format for each one is as follows:

Purpose

This outlines the mathematical objectives of the pupils' pages for the particular chapter.

Materials

This lists all the materials required by the pupils as they work through the mathematics.

Vocabulary

This provides you with the essential mathematical vocabulary that is used in the pupils' books. You will know which words the children will be meeting and be able to introduce them during earlier teaching sessions.

Teaching points

This section contains possible teaching approaches and activities for all the mathematics in the pupils' books. Many of these are introductory activities for the concepts. As well as activities, the notes are full of ideas and games to add to your own approach and already successful methods. You will also find ideas for mental skills, such as a quick way to add 9, that will help children master and enjoy mathematics.

The Cockcroft report emphasises the importance of discussion between teacher and child, and between children. These notes give you suggestions for questions to set discussion going, and give children the opportunity to talk, ask questions and develop their mathematics. It also allows you to listen to the children and see how their understanding is developing.

There are also ideas for introducing the practical activities and further suggestions for developing these.

Using the calculator

In this part there are ideas for incorporating a calculator into mathematics. The calculator is to be used at your discretion and there will be occasions when you won't want the children to use one. However, you will probably want to have calculators readily available and there will be times when children will need a calculator to help them complete their work. The calculator is a useful aid for children to develop a particular piece of mathematics. In the pupils' book a logo is used to indicate where a calculator will be especially useful.

Links with the environment

These notes show how the mathematical ideas may be related to the everyday environment or linked to other curriculum areas. You can develop these ideas further and incorporate them into topic work across the curriculum. The project booklets will also be useful in developing many of these ideas.

Notes on investigations

Investigations are essentially open-ended situations where different approaches can be made. The notes are not meant to be used rigidly but to give guidance and suggestions for developing the mathematics. There is an additional section on investigations included in the introduction (pages 10–11).

ISSUES IN MATHEMATICS TEACHING

Language in mathematics

Language gives mathematics context and meaning. It sets the scene, poses problems and gives information. But the way language is used and how children interpret it is crucial to their success and progress. How then does language affect mathematics?

The words used are important. Some are found only in mathematics and have to be learned, like 'parallelogram' and 'right-angle'. Some, like 'add' and 'equal', have the same meaning in or out of mathematics, and some, the ones most likely to cause problems, have different meanings according to their context; 'table' and 'difference' have both mathematical and ordinary English meanings.

Not only are the words important but so is the style of writing. There will be *explanations* of concepts, methods, vocabulary, notation and rules. *Instructions* will tell the reader what to do, and *exercises* will give practice of the skills and set problems or investigations. *Peripheral text* will introduce exercises or give clues to ways of approach, and *signals* give structure to the text with headings, letters, numbers, boxes and logos. Children must be able to see their way through all these forms of writing.

But, in addition to the words and writing, mathematics also involves reading visual information. A good mathematics text should use illustrations effectively to add information. They should not be purely for decoration, or related but not essential to the mathematics. There are also many forms of visual language which children need to understand. These include tables, graphs, diagrams, plans and maps. It is important to teach children to decode this information, interpret and make use of it, and present their answers or conclusions in different forms.

The skills children need for reading mathematics have only been touched on here. An awareness of the complexities involved will help you to overcome any difficulties caused by language and so prevent them becoming mathematical problems too. Useful books to read are *Children Reading Mathematics*, by Hilary Shuard and Andrew Rothery (John Murray) and *Maths Talk*, from The Mathematical Association.

Mathematics and special needs

Many difficulties which children experience with mathematics are not genuinely mathematical. Children with special educational needs, for whatever reasons, may have problems with mathematics because of a wide variety of factors. By looking at possible causes of difficulty many problems can be prevented or at least significantly helped.

In writing Cambridge Primary Mathematics careful attention has been given to making the mathematics accessible to *all* children, particularly in the A sections. The following areas have been looked at carefully.

Mathematical language

- Familiar words
- Words in context
- Repetition of important words and phrases
- Clear and unambiguous instructions
- Clear indication of response expected
- Sentences of a suitable length and structure
- Clear and unambiguous symbols

Presentation

- Appropriate quantity of work
- Interesting and relevant illustrations
- Variety of presentation
- Attractive page layout to encourage a positive attitude

Independence

- Clear indication of apparatus needed
- Materials that will be readily available
- Instructions children will be able to read and understand

Recording

- No unnecessary writing
- Minimum writing to help children with motor-control difficulties
- Word prompts to aid spelling

Practical work

- Plenty of practical activities
- Use of concrete apparatus encouraged
- Practical work encouraged and built in to the maths

Attitude

- Children are given a purpose to their work
- The mathematics is put in meaningful contexts
- Mathematics is related to other curriculum areas

There are some aspects of special needs that can only be dealt with by you in the classroom. For example, children may not be able to get all the equipment they need and so labelling boxes and drawers with pictures can help. Sometimes their handwriting can cause problems through poor letter or number formation, or because they are left-handed, and extra practice in this may be needed.

Skill support masters for section A give extra support and reinforcement for those children needing further practice or consolidation. Where possible, alternative methods of approach have been given but the masters are essentially to strengthen work already done.

Mathematical language, presentation, independence, recording, practical work and, just as important, the attitude children bring to their work are all vital for success. By identifying whether a difficulty is genuinely mathematical you can remove or alleviate many problems. You know your children best, and by looking at all the factors affecting their learning you can meet their special needs. By doing so, you can give them a love and fascination for mathematics so that they achieve to the best of their potential.

English as a second language in mathematics

Research suggests that many children lack a firm grasp of the language of mathematics. In the case of children with English as a second language, this is often compounded by other language difficulties.

All pupils need the opportunity to hear and use the correct mathematical vocabulary. They need to develop concepts and the appropriate language together. You should not assume that because children can perform a mechanical mathematical task that they understand the associated language. You can check this by discussion with the pupil.

Practical activities are the essential starting point for any topic. Every opportunity should be taken to use correct mathematical vocabulary with pupils and to encourage them to use it when talking with other children and teachers. Where possible this vocabulary should be reinforced in other curricular areas, e.g. art and craft, games, PE etc.

Activities which offer opportunities for group work are also very useful for language development since the children are required to cooperate and to discuss the work they are doing. Investigations, calculator and computer work all lend themselves to pair or group activities.

When discussing work or activities with the children you should try to avoid the questioning approach which only requires short or one-word answers. Instead excourage full explanations of pupils' thoughts and actions using the correct vocabulary.

Weaknesses in mathematical language and the comprehension of mathematical texts often only become apparent in the junior school where greater emphasis is placed on reading and recording. Even pupils who can read a mathematical text may well be unable to interpret it. Oral discussion, individually or in groups, will help to develop the skills required.

Special attention should be given to words which sound similar; for example, 'hundred' 'hundredth', and 'seventeen' 'seventy'.

Pronunciation is often a problem with second-language learners because certain sounds may not exist in their mother tongue. However, they should be encouraged to attempt to make the distinctions clear.

Words which have a different meaning mathematically than in normal English usage – like 'similar', 'different' and 'table' – also need special attention.

It is important not to skimp on the language aspect of mathematics in order to 'push on' with mechanical exercises and recording. A weak language base will lead to downfalls later.

Mathematics and gender

There is evidence that in the past many girls have under-achieved in mathematics. The reasons for this are complex and only an indication can be given here. Although the problem may only become apparent in the secondary school, the roots of it can often lie in the primary school.

In this course there has been an attempt to produce material which will encourage girls as much as boys. As far as is possible, the pupil materials show equal numbers of girls and boys, show them participating equally in all types of activity, and illustrate how mathematics can be used in situations familiar to girls as well as to boys.

However, the written materials are only a part of the mathematics teaching. There is a great deal that you, as a teacher, can do to help the girls in your class.

- Try to encourage the girls in your class to use apparatus and toys which encourage spatial awareness, for example, Lego. Girls often have less access to this kind of toy at home, and an intuitive feeling for space is important for later work.
- Try to make sure that you spend as much time interacting with girls as with boys. It is very easy to give more time to a group of demanding boys and to leave a group of quiet girls to get on with their work.
- There has been research which shows that girls in primary schools are less likely than boys to have a calculator, to own a digital watch and to have a microcomputer at home. You may find it useful to do a survey of your class so that you are aware of the children who may need extra help with these items.

If you would like to find out more about encouraging girls to achieve their potential in mathematics, then you may find it useful to read *Girls into Mathematics* by the Open University (published by Cambridge University Press). The book was mainly written for teachers in secondary schools, but many of the activities could be adapted easily for use in primary schools.

Using the calculator

Calculators are now widely available and are used extensively in the world of work. It is therefore important that children should learn to use them intelligently. The course has been written on the assumption that children have calculators available, although the extent to which they are used is left to the individual teacher.

In the pupils' books a logo is used to show activities which would particularly benefit from the use of a calculator. The teaching notes contain suggestions to develop use of the calculator including many ideas for games.

A simple four-function calculator is all that is required for the early part of this course. Ideally these should be to hand whenever children are doing mathematics and it should be natural for children to turn to them when they are needed. Children with special needs may need to use a calculator to complete section A even in places where the logo is not shown.

The use of the calculator has brought about a shift in the content of the mathematics included in the course. There is less emphasis on straight computation and more on problem-solving. It is also important that children develop mental strategies so that they can check that calculator answers are approximately correct and they have not miskeyed. Ideas for developing these mental skills are given in the teaching notes.

Using the computer

The computer is a useful tool for developing mathematical ideas. It can also be a useful way to get children to discuss their mathematics.

Make the most of any opportunities you have for using the computer during mathematics. Children should work at it in twos or threes as this allows scope for discussion. It is important that within each group, there is no one child dominating and restricting the participation of the others. For this reason it may be necessary to select the groups carefully.

Ideas for using the computer with Module 4 are given in the chapter on using the computer on pages 12–20. This chapter was written by Anita Straker who has a lot of experience in this area. The ideas are not restricted to any particular model of computer.

There is software planned for use alongside the course. The aim of it is to develop problem-solving skills. It is not tied to any particular chapters of the course.

Investigations

Investigations are essentially open-ended activities where children may devise various approaches. They provide an ideal opportunity for children to devise their own pieces of mathematics, to use logical reasoning, and to discuss mathematics between themselves.

Ideally children should work on investigations in small groups. This gives them the chance to talk, think and express their ideas. When they have worked on an investigation as a group for a while, it can be very beneficial to have the group report to the rest of the class on how they approached the task. This gives an opportunity for the class to see alternative approaches and various problem-solving techniques.

It is important not to make remarks that judge children's contributions and not to become so involved that the investigation ceases to be child's. The ideal contribution from the teacher is questions such as:

'Why did this work?'
'Will it work with other shapes or numbers?'
'What would happen if . . .?'

The teaching notes include comments on the investigations. These are not meant to be used rigidly but merely to give some indication of where the investigation might lead. Other approaches may be just as good, or better! Children should be encouraged to find their own way of recording and to ask further questions in order to extend their work.

Algorithms

Algorithms are methods for doing calculations. On the whole, these detailed methods are not given in the texts in order to allow freedom of choice. You can introduce your preferred method, or alternatively the children can devise their own. If children do work out their own algorithms then a teaching approach similar to investigations can be used with children sharing their ideas. This approach has the advantage that the method becomes the child's own and they are more likely to remember it.

Use of practical work

Children should be encouraged to use apparatus and concrete materials whenever possible. It is important that children have plenty of experience in practical situations before moving on to doing more abstract activities. They should not be hurried into making this step.

The materials required for this course are widely available. A checklist of what you will need for Module 4 is given in the appendix.

USING THE COMPUTER

The computer's contribution to children's mathematical work comes through using:

- specific programs in which children can explore mathematical ideas
- adventure games and simulations which support mathematics across the curriculum
- software tools like databases and programming languages which support open-ended problem-solving

In each case, the software can act as a stimulus to children to talk about mathematical ideas. Through their informal discussion with each other and with their teacher even the youngest children can start to build sound intuitive ideas about mathematical concepts. Children need to work in small groups at the computer, so that they have a chance to share and to talk about what is happening on the screen.

Specific programs

Although there are many 'drill and practice' mathematics programs, there seems little point in using the computer for practice when there is already an abundance of mathematics practice material in books, on workcards and on worksheets.

Some of the most attractive of the specific programs are in the form of strategic games of puzzles. In these the children need to focus on the strategy which is to be used, and they will often use mental skills in the process. It is important that teachers link the use of these programs to the children's work away from the keyboard: both preliminary and follow-up activities need to be planned in advance.

There are also specific programs which encourage mathematical investigation. The starting point of the investigation should be through practical work away from the computer, but when the diagrams become too complicated, or the calculations too difficult, the computer program can take over.

Adventure games and simulations

Adventure games, based on fantasy, and simulations, based on fact, give children opportunities to solve problems across the curriculum in a context of fact or fantasy. Simulations like *Cars in Motion* (Cambridge Software House) or *Suburban Fox* (Newman College) require strategic thinking and planning, and the use of a range of mathematical and other skills. Adventure games, like *The Lost Frog* (ESM), *Dread Dragon*

Droom (RESOURCE), *Puff* or *Martello* (A. Straker), all have a series of mathematical puzzles and problems which need to be resolved.

Primary children often lack confidence in problem-solving situations but such programs can provide them with additional opportunities for developing their mathematical thinking and increasing their range of problem-solving strategies. The role of the teacher in encouraging discussion about the possible forms of solution is an important one here. Questions like 'What would happen if instead . . .?', or 'How many different ways could we . . .?', or 'Would it be possible to . . .?', all help to extend the children's thinking about a particular problem.

Databases

Databases support a range of statistical work across the curriculum. Databases can be used to encourage the children to ask questions, to collect, organise and analyse data, and to find patterns and relationships.

There are two kinds of databases which are useful.

Sorting Game (MESU), *Seek* (Longman) and *Branch* (MEP Project Work Pack) are databases based upon a branching-tree structure. They encourage the use of very precise mathematical description in sorting and classifying. Children can set up binary-tree classification systems, using the program alongside the practical sorting activities which take place throughout the primary school.

Databases like *Our Facts* (MESU) or *Factfile* (CUP) work in the same way as a card index system. Graph drawing packages like *Picfile* (CUP), which display the data graphically, are very helpful here.

Programming

Young children begin 'to program' as soon as they start to find ways of recording things like a sequence of moves in a game, the commands to give to a battery-driven robot, or the shapes which are needed to make up a picture. A computer program, like a sheet of music or a knitting pattern, is simply a set of precise, coded instructions arranged in an appropriate order, and programming is another way in which children can use the computer as a tool to explore mathematical ideas.

The programming language which is most often used in primary schools is Logo. The point of introducing young children to programming with Logo is to allow them to feel in control, to give them a way of clarifying their ideas, and to encourage them to order their thoughts logically. Although the children will need to be taught some simple programming techniques, the emphasis needs to be not on learning these techniques, but on the mathematics that can be explored through programming.

Stage 1

Addition and subtraction

Computer software can help to provide practice with the ordering of two-digit numbers: for example

- *Boxes* (MicroSMILE): ten random numbers must be placed in a line of boxes so that they are in order.
- *Find Me* (MEP Primary Maths): children must guess a number using clues of 'too big' or 'too small'.

Computer games and puzzles are also helpful for providing practice in simple addition and subtraction with numbers to 20 in a setting which involves the development of strategy: for example

- *Toyshop* (MEP Infant Pack): players take turns to pay a coin towards the cost of a toy costing up to 20 pence – the player who pays the last coin is the winner.
- *Counters* (Micros in the Primary Classroom – Longman): players take turns to place a counter on a 1–1 number line – the winner is the first player to make fifteen with any three counters.
- *Line Up* (Number Games – A. Straker): a number showing on a dice indicates how many counters can be placed in a frame numbered cne to six (for example, if 6 is rolled then 6 may be filled in, or two 3s, or three 2s, or 1 and 2 and 3).

Multiplication and division

Some computer games and puzzles are helpful for providing practice in simple multiplication and division in a setting which involves the development of strategy: for example

- *Jane Plus* (Longman): the teacher can determine the 'rule' in a function box, and the children must guess what is happening.

There are also simple investigations which children can carry out with the aid of the computer to collect data: for example

- *Tiles 1* (Mathematical Investigations: Capital Media): a row of blue tiles is surrounded by a single line of red tiles, and the children try to investigate the general rule that connects the number of blue tiles with the number of red tiles.

Data

If the children have been doing a project about themselves then they can create a simple database like *Our Facts* (MESU) to record and display the information which they have collected.

For example, they might have measured their heights and other body measurements in hand spans, or in pencil lengths. Each child could make a record:

NAME

AGE (years)

SEX

HEIGHT (spans)

REACH (spans)

When all the information has been entered, the children can display it on a Venn diagram, or on a pictogram, to answer their questions. Are there more boys than girls? Who is the tallest, and who is the shortest? Who has the middle height? What is the most common height? Does there seem to be a connection between height and reach?

Angle

Computer software can provide opportunities for using commands of left or right to change direction: for example

- *Treasure Hunt* (MEP Infant Pack) is a simple adventure game with three main locations: the teacher operates the keyboard and involves the children in discussion about the direction to take to find the treasure, encouraging them to use language like up, down, left, right.

Activities with programmable toys and battery-driven floor robots also help to develop ideas about left and right, clockwise and anti-clockwise. Ideas for what a battery-driven robot might be made to do can of course be suggested by the teacher, but the best suggestions have to come from the children themselves. Some ideas are teaching the robot to . . .

- go to the top of the slope and stop
- move in a circle
- go all round the table and back to us again
- zig-zag through the bean bags
- make the waves on the sea
- do a dance with another robot

Encourage the children to make their own suggestions for what they will try to get the robot to do.

Shape

Computer software can provide opportunities for building shapes and patterns, and for discovering the relationships which enable one shape to be placed next to another: for example

- *Picture Maker* (ESM): pictures can be built up using eight colours, five shapes, and four movements.
  Mosaics (MEP Infant Pack): mosaic patterns made from squares of varying sizes can be designed and printed.

Stage 2

Addition and subtraction

Computer software can help to provide practice with the concepts of place value: for example

- *Size Game* (MEP Primary Maths): the players must try to make a number of 3, 4 or 5 digits which is larger (or smaller) than the one which the computer makes.
- *Counter* (ATM): a starting number can be set, and a step size, so that patterns of digits can be explored – the sound which can be placed separately on each of the units, tens and hundreds digits is an attractive feature.

Using *Counter*, there are a number of questions to explore.

- If the counter starts at 3, and the step size is 5, will it land on 53? Will it land on 77?
- Can you explain the patterns in the units digits when the counter counts in fives? How many different units digits occur when it counts in fours? How many occur when it counts in twos? Can you explain this?

Number games and puzzles are helpful for providing practice in addition and subtraction of single-digit numbers to or from a two-digit total in a setting which involves the development of strategy.

- *Play Train* (MEP Infant Pack): the carriages on a train must be filled with people to total the number on the engine.
- *Chains* (Number Games – A. Straker): numbers are 'picked up' as you travel through a grid – the aim is to acquire a target number.
- *Cranky* (EMS): children solve calculator-style number puzzles using only certain digits and signs.

Multiplication and division

Some computer games and puzzles are helpful for providing practice in multiplication and division in a setting which involves the development of strategy: for example

- *Happy Time* (Shiva Numeracy 4 – ESM): racing your opponent to the planet practises the use of 2, 3, 4 and 5 times tables.

Data

There are several different programs which encourage children to develop ideas of position as an introduction to the use of coordinates.

- *Albert's House* (ESM): children take Albert the mouse on an adventure to discover what is inside his house.
- *Lost Frog* (ESM): children need to devise a simple way of keeping track of their position as they try to recover the frog and restore it to its home in the garden.

Angle

Computer software can extend opportunities for using left and right commands, and concepts of a whole turn, half turn or quarter turn: for example.

- *Maze* (MicroSMILE): the problem is to trace a path through a randomly generated maze – some children find it difficult to realise that they need to turn left if they are pointing down the screen and want to move to its right-hand-side.
- *Crash* (MEP Microprimer): the children need to give a series of forward and turning instructions in order to get round an obstacle course.

Shape

Computer software can provide opportunities for building three-dimensional objects in an exploratory way: for example

- *Build* (MEP Microprimer): children can design three-dimensional structures made from cubes – they can make some from Multilink first, and then try to produce the design on the screen, or they can try to make with Multilink the structure which appears in two-dimensional form on the screen.

Stage 3

Addition and subtraction

The use of computer software provides opportunities to explore number patterns, which helps with the concepts of place value: for example

- *Spots* (Number Games – A. Straker): two numbers in a pattern of seven numbers are already filled in, and the problem is to fill the gaps.
- *Ergo* (MEP Microprimer): a pattern of numbers hidden on a square grid must be discovered with the help of 'too big' or 'too small' clues.
- *Monty* (ATM): the python called Monty wriggles around on a number grid, and the challenge is to find the numbers that he is covering up.

Computer games and puzzles are helpful for providing practice in addition and subtraction with numbers up to 100 in a setting which involves the development of strategy.

- *Target* (Mathematical Games and Activities: Capital Media): each player has a set of counters numbered 1 to 9 which can be used once each to put towards a total.
- *Make 37* (Number games – A. Straker): by sliding around and across a grid of five numbers, the players accumulate numbers towards a total of 37.

- *Number Painter* (ESM): a painter has to be moved up and down ladders collecting numbers as he does so to make your target.

The activities which children do on a calculator can also be done on a computer. After they have learned how to add two numbers together on their calculator they can use either BASIC or Logo and type in

PRINT 6 + 9

to see the result on the screen. They can try a group of operations:

PRINT 7 + 5 − 3 + 17

They can make comparisons:

PRINT 23 + 41 compared with PRINT 41 + 23

Using the PRINT command, they can explore some problems. For example, how many different ways are there for adding numbers together to make 15? What numbers can be made by adding together a pair of consecutive numbers?

Multiplication and division

Computer games and puzzles are helpful for providing practice in multiplication and division in a setting which involves the development of strategy: for example

- *Blocks* (MEP Primary Maths): the three digits shown by three rolling dice can be used in any combination, together with signs and symbols, to block out a number on a grid. The object is to block out four numbers in a row.

The activities which children do on a calculator can also be done on a computer. After they have learned how to add, subtract, multiply or divide the numbers together on their calculator they can type in

PRINT 6 * 2   or   PRINT 15 / 3

to see the result on the computer screen. (The asterisk * is used for a multiplication sign, and the slash / for a division sign.) They can make comparisons:

PRINT 3 * 4   compared with   PRINT 4 * 3

and try combinations of operations:

PRINT 2 + 3 * 4   or   PRINT 2 * 3 + 4

and repeated operations:

PRINT 5 + 5 + 5 + 5 + 5 + 5 + 5   or   PRINT 7 * 5

They can try challenges. For example, what set of numbers can be made by adding three consecutive whole numbers?

As with the calculator, children exploring division will discover numbers like 2·5 or 4·333 333 33. If children express curiosity, then repeat the operation, but using Unifix cubes. For example, a child who has tried PRINT 5 / 2, can also try dividing five Unifix cubes into two piles. The last cube will need to be exchanged for one made of plasticine, which can be cut in half. 2·5 can be explained as the way that the computer 'writes' two and a half.

Data

If the children have been doing a project about themselves then they can create a simple database like *Our Facts* (MESU) to record and display the information which they have collected.

For example, they might have measured their heights in metres, and their body weight in kilograms, their leg length in centimetres and a run time for 50 metres in seconds. Each child could make a record:

NAME

AGE (years)

SEX

HEIGHT (m)

WEIGHT (kg)

LEG LENGTH (cm)

RUN TIME (s)

When all the information has been entered, the children can display it in a block graph or scattergram to help to answer their questions. Are boys taller than girls? What is the middle (median) weight of the class? Does there seem to be a connection between leg length and run time?

Angle

Logo is a computer language which young children can use almost as soon as they can count and recognise simple written words. The easy way for them to start is a method of drawing lines to make pictures or patterns called *turtle graphics* or *turtle geometry*.

The lines are drawn on the screen by a small arrow, called a screen turtle, or on the floor by a small robot on wheels, called a floor turtle. Some floor turtles are connected to the computer by a long cable; others receive an infra-red signal from a small piece of equipment which is plugged into the computer. Between the turtle's wheels is a pen holder, which can either be up or down. When it is down, then the turtle will trace a line as it moves.

The turtle can be moved using four simple commands: FORWARD and BACKWARD (to make it move in those directions), and LEFT and

RIGHT (to make it turn on the spot). Each command needs to be followed by a number to determine the amount which is to be moved or turned.

Nimbus Logo	BBC Logotron	
FORWARD (FD)	FORWARD (FD)	These four
BACKWARD (BK)	BACK (BK)	commands need
RIGHT (RT)	RIGHT (RT)	to be followed by
LEFT (LT)	LEFT (LT)	a number
LIFT	PEN UP (PU)	
DROP	PEN DOWN (PD)	

Children often begin their work with Logo in PE activities, in which they explore space through body movements of left and right, or forwards and backwards. They continue this by experimenting as one child gives the instructions, and another tries to make a line drawing, or to trace a path through a maze. The work with the turtle usually starts by the children designing maze games or target games on the floor – can I get the turtle to go round these three skittles and back to me?

Shape

Logo is an ideal way of producing simple pictures or patterns using properties of length or distance, and angle. Suggest: Can you make a square? Can you make a window? Can you make a set of steps? Encourage the children to suggest their own ideas, and remember to allow enough time at the keyboard for each group to explore the ideas to the full.

Computer software can provide opportunities for exploring lines of symmetry.

Programmable toys can be operated so that they carry out one action at a time, but they can also store a complete sequence of instructions to be carried out continuously. Two floor robots can be programmed to 'dance' with each other about a line of symmetry.

Logo can also be used to explore ideas of line symmetry. For example, if the turtle draws a pattern of lines on one side of the screen, what commands are needed to make the mirror image of the pattern on the other side of the screen?

Fractions

The computer program *Halving*, in the MEP Primary Mathematics Pack, can provide a stimulus to an investigation into finding the many different ways in which a square may be halved.

TEACHING NOTES

Number 1

Purpose

- To revise number bonds to 20
- To revise the commutative property, e.g. $2 + 3 = 3 + 2$
- To revise or introduce place value to tens and units
- To revise the addition of tens and units without exchange or 'carrying'

Materials

Number lines, structural apparatus, squared paper, calculator, spike abacus

Vocabulary

Double, add, equals, calculator, pattern, display, button, keyboard, window, cancel, score, pairs, abacus

TEACHING POINTS

1 Everyday numbers

Talk with the children about numbers.
'Where do we see numbers?' Houses, cars, etc.
'Why do we use numbers?' To count; to know amounts; to know positions of objects like houses; we like to know the date of our birthday; we need to count our money, etc.
   Revise the vocabulary of 'greater than', 'fewer than'.
4 is one greater than 3.
3 is one fewer than 4.
   Where else do the children see numbers? Buses, football results, shops. Make them aware of how numbers surround them.
   The idea of pattern in number is important. Encourage children to look for it.

2 Number patterns and mental work

Adding 1, 2, 3 to numbers, pointing out the patterns.
Doubling numbers, e.g. $1 + 1, \ldots, 10 + 10$.
Adding 10 to particular numbers.
Adding 9 to particular numbers $(+ 10 - 1)$.
   Show the commutative property: $2 + 3 = 3 + 2$.

Let children practise with numbers. Let them play with numbers on card, on the board, with magnetic numbers, etc. Make numbers fun!

3 Number line

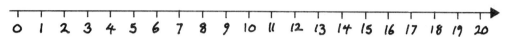

Have a large demonstration wall number line or give children individual number lines.

Show how addition is done on the number line and how to record it.

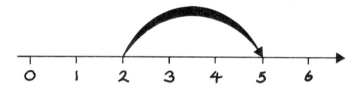

Start on 2, move 3 spaces and land on 5.

For fun, you can introduce a creature that hops or jumps, such as Freda the frog, or Ken the kangaroo.

4 Doubling

Play a 'doubling' game. Flash cards are placed face downwards on the table. A card is turned over by the teacher and held up. The number is doubled and recorded on paper, e.g. 7 + 7 = 14.

Talk about when children double numbers in Scrabble, darts or board games, for example.

5 Place value

Place value needs to be reinforced constantly. Use whatever methods suit you best. Unifix, Centicube or squared paper are suitable.

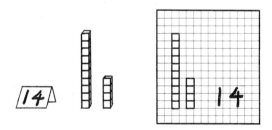

Cards are useful to demonstrate place value.

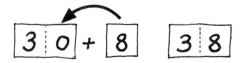

'What is this number?' 38
'What does the 3 stand for?' 3 tens = 30

'What does the 8 stand for?' 8 units = 8
'So 38 is 3 tens and 8 units.'
   Play a game either in pairs or in groups, using cards.
'What is 40 + 2?' 42
'What is 43?' 40 + 3
Other games like Snap, Pairs or dominoes can be played.

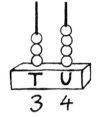

6 Spike abacus

The spike abacus is used for place value practice. Let the children show TU numbers on an abacus, using real ones or on paper.

7 Recording

The recording method used here is vertical recording. Use structural apparatus to provide concrete practice for the children. This practical work is necessary for them to build up images of number work in their minds. (You may find they need practice in changing from a horizontal to a vertical form of recording.)

T	U

$$33 + 24 \rightarrow \begin{array}{r} T\ U \\ 33 \\ +\ 24 \\ \hline 57 \end{array}$$

Make 'place value' boards like the one above. Use an A4 sized piece of thin card. Mark the lines and TU. Cover the cards with transparent covering to protect them. These boards will be useful in all number work.

USING THE CALCULATOR   Remember – calculators vary in the way they work.

1 Explore the keyboard

First let children explore the calculator keyboard:

- Looking at the sequence of numbers
- Looking at number patterns on the keyboard
- Noticing that 'opposite' numbers add up to 10
- Noticing that odd numbers are at the corners

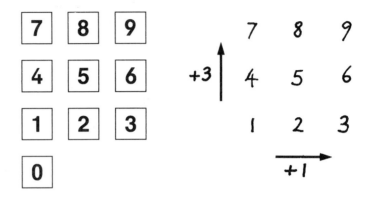

If you don't have enough calculators, the keyboard can be duplicated for use in a class lesson or discussion.

2 Basic skills

If children are not familiar with using calculators, talk about the basic skills:

- How to switch on the calculator
- The 'window display'
- How to enter a number
- How to use the CANCEL button, rather than the ON/OFF switch

3 Number bonds

Let the children practise simple number bonds, e.g. 3 + 5.

Switch on the calculator.

Press the ⌶3⌷.

Press the ⌶+⌷.

Press the ⌶5⌷.

Press the ⌶=⌷.

Read off the answer.

4 Two-digit numbers

Practise entering two-digit numbers, and let the children try adding numbers up to 20.

5 Number patterns

Talk about patterns obtained by repeated addition, for example,

2 4 6 8 10 12 14 16 18 20

Children may often use the calculator to aid the investigation at the end of each section, and in many other parts of the work.

A game to play

Enter a given number. You have to get to exactly 20 in one, two or three moves. For example,

15 + 5 = 20   or   15 + 3 + 2 = 20   or   15 + 2 + 2 + 1 = 20

LINKS WITH THE ENVIRONMENT

Ask children to look for numbers on the way to school. Ask them for the largest/smallest one- or two-digit number they can find.

Talk about games where a player's or team's score goes up one point each time like quiz games or soccer. Cricket scores go up in ones, fours and sixes. Think about other games like snooker, hockey, rugby, etc.

Encourage the children to become 'number spotters'.

NOTES ON INVESTIGATIONS

Section A

Ask children how they approached the problem.

Are numbers merely picked at random? Do children attempt to structure their approach in any way? For example, do they first try 1 + ☐, then 2 + ☐, then 3 + ☐.

Do they devise a system of recording or crossing off numbers that have been used?

X̸ 2̸ 3̸ 4 5 6 7 8 9̸ 1̸0̸   1 + 10 = 11
                                        2 + 9 = 11
                                        3 + . . .

Section B

Do the children understand what is involved in producing a pattern? Do they appreciate that when there is a pattern, it is possible to forecast the next term? Do they, for example, add the *same* number each time?

Do any children use a calculator to help them? How might the constant function on a calculator be used to make a number pattern?

Section C

This is more demanding and some children are likely to adopt a trial-

and-error approach initially. Is there a possible system? For example, start with 1 and work along the line:

1 + 2 + ☐ =   No number large enough
1 + 3 + ☐ =   No number large enough
1 + 4 + ☐ =   No number large enough
1 + 5 + 9 = 15   It works! So far anyway

Now start with 2, etc.

    This is one way to show the answer.

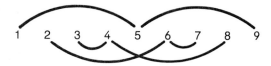

This investigation might be extended to using the numbers 1 to 11 and three boxes with 22 on each, or 1 to 12 with 26 on each box.

Number 2

Purpose

- To revise subtraction number bonds to 20
- To revise place value to tens and units
- To revise subtraction of tens and units without exchange or 'carrying'

Materials

Number lines, structural apparatus, place-value boards

Vocabulary

Take away, difference, subtract, pairs, missing signs

TEACHING POINTS   **1 Number line**

It is helpful to have a large demonstration wall number line and give children individual ones. Show subtraction by 'jumping' back along the number line and discuss how to record it.

'Start on 7, jump back 4 spaces and land on 3.'

2 Vocabulary

Revise the words 'take away' and 'subtract'. Show how to take away using cubes or counters. For example:
'Six take away two leaves four.'
'6 subtract 2 equals 4.'
'6 − 2 = 4'

Revise or introduce the word 'difference'. Show the 'difference' using cubes.

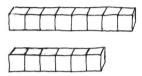

'The difference between 8 and 6 is 2.'
'8 − 6 = 2'

Children need to be familiar with this vocabulary. Play games, make up stories and give lots of practice so that the words become a natural part of their mathematics vocabulary.

A game to play

Pick 10 children to play. Call out a difference, e.g. 'difference of 2'. The children get into groups with a difference of 2. Play again, using a different 10 children.

3 Mental work

Set puzzles for the children using numbers of objects in the room. For example:
'Add the number of legs of three tables; take away the number of legs of one child.'
'Add the number of lights and the number of doors; subtract the number of ears of one child.'

Adapt these to suit your class; it is very good for mental mathematics.

4 Place value of tens and units

Use dot pictures.

Use counters on a place-value board. (Place-value boards can be easily made from card.)

Use structural apparatus.

Use number cards.

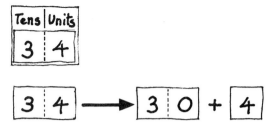

These are all practical and useful ways of illustrating place value.

5 Recording

The recording method shown here is vertical recording. Use structural apparatus to subtract tens and units. This helps children to build up images of numbers.

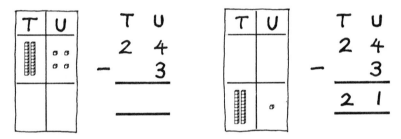

Start building an awareness that forms of recording can be different, but the answers are the same. For example,

46 − 13 = 33
```
     T  U
     4  6
  -  1  3
     3  3
```

USING THE CALCULATOR   Revise basic procedures if necessary. See pages 23–5.

1 Subtraction bonds

Let the children practise simple subtraction bonds, e.g. 8 − 3.

Switch on the calculator.

Press the 8 .

Press the − .

Press the 3 .

Press the = .

Read off the answer.

2 Two-digit subtraction

Show the children how to enter two-digit numbers. Let them practise subtraction of numbers up to 20.

A game to play

Enter 20. You have to get to 14 in one, two or three moves. For example,
$20 - 6 = 14$ or $20 - 2 - 4 = 14$ or $20 - 2 - 1 - 3 = 14$

LINKS WITH THE ENVIRONMENT   Talk with the children about subtraction situations in everyday life. These might include:

- knocking tins off a shelf at a fairground or fête
- eating sweets one at a time
- eating a cake piece by piece
- the countdown for a spaceship launch or on a microwave oven
- the number of seconds left to answer questions during TV quiz shows

NOTES ON INVESTIGATIONS

Section A

Do the children use their first pair of numbers with a difference of 3 to find other pairs? For example,

$$4 - 1, \quad 5 - 2, \quad 6 - 3$$

Are they systematic in finding all the possibilities?
    The investigation can be extended to finding other differences.

Section B

Some children may choose any of the numbers and try to find all the possibilities in a random way. However, the problem may be approached in a more-systematic manner by exhausting one number before going to the next. A diagram might be helpful.

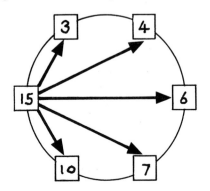

Section C

Do the children use the first pair of numbers and then find other pairs with the same difference? For example,

$$10 - 9 = 1, \quad 9 - 8 = 1, \quad 8 - 7 = 1, \quad \text{etc.}$$

Are they systematic in finding all the possibilities?
It might be helpful for some children if the numbers are written on separate pieces of paper.

shape 1

Purpose

- To revise or introduce the square, rectangle, circle, triangle, hexagon and pentagon
- To consider their properties
- To relate these shapes to the environment

Materials

Equilateral triangles, squares, pentagons, rectangles, hexagons, circles, squared paper, copy of the Highway Code

Vocabulary

Square, rectangle, circle, triangle, hexagon, pentagon, corner, side, equilateral, sign, pattern, shape

TEACHING POINTS   ## 1 Looking at shapes

Begin the topic by holding up shapes and asking questions like:
'What is the name of this shape?'
'Can you see it in the classroom?'
'How many corners does it have?'
'How many sides does it have?'
'Are there the same number of sides as corners?'

2 The circle

Look at a circle – are there any corners? Point out that there are only corners when straight lines meet.

3 Regular shapes

Tell the children to look at these regular shapes.

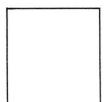 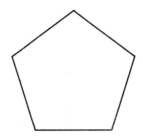 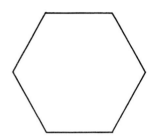

Ask questions like
'Are all sides the same length?'
'Are all corners the same size?'
   Help children to realise that all the sides and all the angles of a
regular shape are the same.

4 Shapes in the environment

Talk about shapes in the environment: in the classroom, in the home,
on the way to school.
   Consider the basic shapes on road signs. Have a 'road sign' quiz.
Look at a copy of the Highway Code. Talk about the significance of the
shape of a road sign.

warning   command   guidance

USING THE CALCULATOR
Although this topic does not always lend itself to calculator work, the
children can solve number puzzles using the properties of shapes.
This type of calculator activity gives practice in deciding which
operation of +, −, ×, ÷ is the correct one to use. Here are two
examples.
(i)   'How many sides do four pentagons have? Can you discover at
      least two ways of finding out, using a calculator?'

e.g. $5 + 5 + 5 + 5 = 20$
       $4 \times 5 = 20$

(ii) 'How many separate triangles could you make from 12 straws?'
      'How many straws altogether?' 12 straws.
      'How many straws are needed to make one triangle?' 3 straws.
      'What do we need to know?' How many threes are in twelve?
      'How do we do this?' We divide.
      'How do we enter this on the calculator?'   [12] [÷] [3] [=]

LINKS WITH THE ENVIRONMENT

Talk about all the shapes in the classroom; e.g. the clockface may be a circle, a table top is a rectangle.

What shapes do the children see on the way to school? You can make an impressive display of these.

Which is the most popular shape?

Talk about why particular shapes are used for certain situations. For example, why are windows usually rectangular? Is it for ease of building, cutting glass to fit?

Build up a collection of pictures showing shapes in bridges, pylons, cranes, etc.

NOTES ON INVESTIGATIONS

Section A

Discuss the name and the properties of the equilateral triangle.
'How many sides are there?'
'What do you notice about each side?'
'How many triangles fit around one triangle?'
Make a shape by placing triangles in a line.

Section B

Discuss the properties of a hexagon and how to draw one on squared paper. Encourage children to try making various patterns. Ask them if it is possible to make a pattern without gaps, and with gaps?

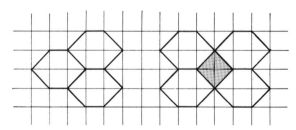

Section C

Notice if the children try to devise a system. Do they explore all the possibilities of one shape before moving on to the next? Do they look for shapes in unfamiliar positions? For example, as well as recognising 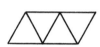 as a triangle, do they also recognise ?

These should be discussed.

The answer is 2 squares, 8 triangles, 7 pentagons.

To extend the activity, children can draw their own pictures.

Number 3

Purpose

- To introduce multiplication as repeated addition
- To show that multiplication is commutative
- To show methods of recording
- To discover number patterns in multiplication

Materials

Number line, squared paper, structural apparatus

Vocabulary

Sets of, pattern, number line, equal groups, graph, pairs, tables

TEACHING POINTS

1 Talking about numbers

Begin by talking about real situations when the same number is repeatedly added: in some games, points or goals are added on; in laying a table, knives and forks are put out; etc.

Use an example of saving a regular amount of pocket money every week, and show how this can be done by addition. For example,

$$10p + 10p + 10p + 10p + 10p = 50p$$

Change the amount of money saved to be relevant to the children.

2 Work with the calculator

Now ask how repeated addition can be done by calculator. One way is to press

$$\boxed{5}\ \boxed{+}\ \boxed{5}\ \boxed{+}\ \boxed{5}\ \boxed{+}\ \ldots$$

Another method is to use the constant function. For example, press

$$\boxed{5}\ \boxed{+}\ \boxed{+}$$

and then press only the $\boxed{=}$ key each time to produce the sequence 5, 10, 15 . . .

    NB   Calculators can vary in their mode of operation. Check for this if the children are using their own calculators.

3 The number line

You can also use number lines for adding. Talk about this with the children.

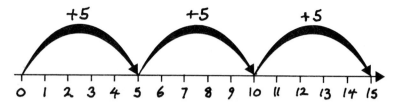

'How many fives have we added together?'
'How many sets of 5 did we add?'

4 Recording

Explain how this can be recorded. For example,

$5 + 5 + 5 = 15$
3 sets of 5 = 15
$3 \times 5 = 15$

Use plenty of examples to help children's imagery. Sets of cards like these can easily be made for practice.

        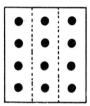

2 + 2 + 2   4 + 4 + 4
3 sets of 2   3 sets of 4
$3 \times 2 = 6$ $3 \times 4 = 12$

Turn the card for children to see the commutative property:

        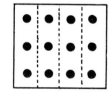

3 + 3   3 + 3 + 3 + 3
2 sets of 3   4 sets of 3
$2 \times 3 = 6$ $4 \times 3 = 12$

5 Commutative property

It is important for children to realise that multiplication is commutative. Let them experiment to see if this always works by drawing or playing with counters or other apparatus. Recording the results is often helpful.

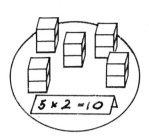
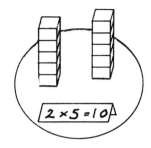

6 Looking for patterns

Squared paper can be used in many ways to show commutativity and pattern. For example, give the children squared paper and ask them to mark out a 1–50 rectangle. This one shows the pattern of 5.

1	2	3	4	5	6	7	8	9	10
11	12	13	14	15	16	17	18	19	20
21	22	23	24	25	26	27	28	29	30
31	32	33	34	35	36	37	38	39	40
41	42	43	44	45	46	47	48	49	50

Look at the ways patterns of 2, 5 and 10 work out on squared paper. Colour in the patterns. They can be checked using calculators.

1	2	3	4	5	6	7	8	9
10	11	12	13	14	15	16	17	18
19	20	21	22	23	24	25	26	27
28	29	30	31	32	33	34	35	36
37	38	39	40	41	42	43	44	45
46	47	48	49	50	51	52	53	54

1	2	3
4	5	6
7	8	9
10	11	12
13	14	15
16	17	18
19	20	21

These are some other ways of writing out patterns on squared paper.

MENTAL WORK Let the children practise the commutative property. Ask 'What is another way of finding 3 sets of 2?' (2 sets of 3)

Ask the children to count on in 2s, 5s, and 10s. This can be done by counting out loud around the class.

Give the children practice in multiplication bonds. For example,

$$3 \times 2 = \square, \ 3 \text{ sets of } 2 = \square$$

USING THE CALCULATOR Revise basic procedures if necessary.

Practise routine operations.

Switch on your calculator.

Press the $\boxed{3}$.

Press the $\boxed{\times}$.

Press the $\boxed{5}$.

Press the $\boxed{=}$.

Read off the answer.

Practise multiplication of 2, 5, 10 up to 50.

Practise building up the tables of 2, 5 and 10 using the constant function for addition; i.e. press $\boxed{2}$ $\boxed{+}$ $\boxed{+}$ to produce 2, 4, 6, 8, 10 . . . (Remember – calculators may vary.) Talk about the patterns that are made.

A game to play

Use the numbers 2, 5, 10 and the $\boxed{\times}$ key as many times as you wish. How many ways can you find to get the answer 20?

LINKS WITH THE ENVIRONMENT Talk about things that come in sets. For example, twos (shoes, socks), threes (traffic lights, legs on stools, tripod legs), fours (wheels on cars, etc.).

Build up tables and graphs to show sets of objects.

Where do we find multiplication appearing in games? Talk about darts where we have doubles and trebles, and Scrabble.

NOTES ON INVESTIGATIONS **Section A**

The real value of this investigation is in the discussion.

Do the children look for a system of attempting the investigation? 'Could we have 1 set of $\square$ = 12?'

'Could we have 2 sets of ☐ = 12?'
'Could we have 3 sets of ☐ = 12?'
'Why can we not have 5 sets?' This might be shown practically and the problem of remainders and fair shares discussed.

Section B

Do the children look for a system?
'Could we have 2 sets, 3 sets, 4 sets, etc.?'
   Do they use the commutative property, e.g. $2 \times 10 = 10 \times 2$?
   The numbers that cannot be grouped are prime numbers – did the children find these? (11, 13, 17, 19)

Section C

Do the children adopt a system? If not, how do they do it?
   Can they do it using just 2? $2 + 2 + 2 + 2 + 2 + 2 + 2 + 2 + 2$. What about $2 \times 2 \times 2 \times 2 + 2$? Are there any more?
   Can they do it using just 3? $3 + 3 + 3 + 3 + 3 + 3$
   Can they do it using 2 and 3?
   Do children consider the commutative property?

Area 1

Purpose

- To introduce ideas of covering surfaces
- To show that the square is one of the best shapes for covering surfaces

Materials

Squared paper, templates of circles, squares, rectangles, equilateral triangles, hexagons, pentagons
   Useful apparatus for class or group work: sheets of newspaper; pages of magazines; paper plates – various sizes are available; large coloured shapes; posters; sheets of sugar paper; large coloured circles or squares.

Vocabulary

square, circle, rectangle, equilateral triangle, hexagon, pentagon, dividing, different

TEACHING POINTS   **1 Looking at surfaces**

Look around the classroom, finding all the different flat surfaces. Are any of the surfaces covered by shapes, e.g. ceiling, wall or floor tiles? Look for gaps between the shapes.

Where else in the school, or at home, are flat shapes fitted together?

2 Using squares

Use a variety of practical activities to introduce covering surfaces. Emphasise that the shapes must touch.

Make up a class set of large squares. These will be useful for class or group activities. (NB Glue velcro on the back to stick them onto fuzzy surfaces or magnetic tape for metal surfaces.) Using squares, talk about the different arrangements that are possible.

 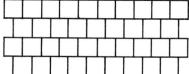

3 Using rectangles

Activity 2 can be repeated with rectangles. Use rectangular pages from a wallpaper pattern book for covering surfaces.

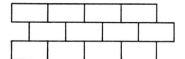  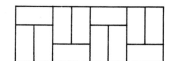

4 Using circles

Now let children make patterns with circles. Talk about the gaps.

 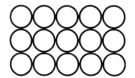

5 Finding the best shape

The children now need to see which is the best shape for covering surfaces. Choose one surface to be covered using squares, rectangles and circles separately. Talk about 'good' and 'bad' things about the shapes. Can the children work out which is the best shape to use? Can they see that the squares fit into corners and can be easily counted?

LINKS WITH THE ENVIRONMENT

At home or school, look for wall, floor or ceiling tiles, wallpaper, and board games – chess, snakes and ladders.

Outside, consider bricks, paving stones, fencing, windows – leaded, small panes – and bridges.

In shops, look at stacked tins or boxes and wrapping paper.

In Clive King's *Stig of the Dump* there is a passage where Barney makes a 'window' using jam jars – a lovely example of how shapes leave gaps. (Chapter 2, pp. 36–8, Copyright Clive King 1963, Puffin books)

NOTES ON INVESTIGATIONS

Section A

How do the children tackle the task? Are they systematic in finding the following shapes?

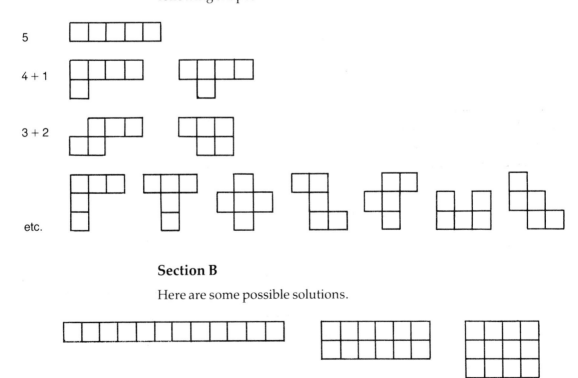

5

4 + 1

3 + 2

etc.

Section B

Here are some possible solutions.

This investigation can be extended by finding shapes other than rectangles made from 12 squares, or by looking for rectangles made from other numbers of squares, such as 15.

Section C

Do the children see that the squares have sides of lengths 1 cm, 2 cm, 4 cm?

The next sized rectangle that can be divided into squares in three different ways is 4 × 12. There are other possibilities beyond this.

Number 4

Purpose

- To revise the concept of division as sharing and grouping
- To revise or introduce the ÷ sign
- To show the link between multiplication and division
- To practise division by 2, 3, 4, 5

Materials

Structural apparatus, squared paper

Vocabulary

Share, group, between, equally, divide, sets, dividing, matches, computer, number sentence.

TEACHING POINTS   **1 Sharing**

Fair shares
Do children understand what is meant by sharing?
'When do we share? What does share mean?'

Explain that sharing can mean when we share a room or a toy. It can also mean sharing a number of things. Then the idea of a 'fair share' is important. For example, if we share six sweets between two children, they each get three. What things might they want to share equally?

Share and record

Use practical examples to show sharing. For example, share 6 marbles between 2 children.

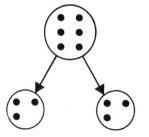
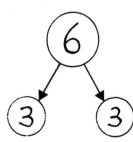

Show the method of recording:

$$6 \div 2 = 3$$

6 shared between 2 gives 3 each

Deal out eight cards to four children. Let them record the result.

$$8 \div 4 = 2$$

8 shared between 4 gives 2 each
Practise sharing using counters, pencils, paper clips, etc.

Number sentences

Look at number sentences such as:

$$12 \div 3 = \square$$
$$12 \div 4 = \square$$

Ask the children to tell you what is happening and to find the answers.

2 Grouping

Revise the idea of grouping, for example,
'How many sets of 4 in 12?'
Link this with such ideas as getting into sets or teams of four in PE: '12 children; how many teams of 4?'
   Group the children in the class:
'I want to see how many groups of 3 there are in 21 children.'
Demonstrate this with the children by moving three of them each time and counting the groups.

Practise grouping using cubes and counters, or any other classroom objects such as pine cones, bottle tops, straws, animal shapes.

A game to play

GRAB A HANDFUL

One child 'grabs' a handful of counters or cubes. If the handful divides exactly into groups of 2, 3, 4 or 5, write a number sentence and score a point.

3 Linking multiplication and division

Use squared paper to show the link between multiplication and division.

1	2
3	4
5	6
7	8
9	10

'How many sets of 2 in 10?'

$10 \div 2 = 5$

There are five sets of two.

$5 \times 2 = 10$

MENTAL WORK   Many of the activities here can be used to practise mental skills.

USING THE CALCULATOR

1 Simple division

Practise simple division.
Switch on your calculator.

Press the 8.
Press the $\div$.
Press the 2.
Press the $=$.

Read off the answer.
Practise dividing by 2, 3, 4 and 5. Set these problems in real situations whenever possible.

2 Remainders

Eventually, as the children experiment with their calculators, the question of remainders will arise and many teachers will feel that this is not the time to discuss decimal notation on the calculator. Instead it may be more appropriate to explain to the children that whole numbers are shown before the point on the calculator. If there are numbers showing after the point (other than 0 on some calculators) this is because the answer is not a whole number and therefore the number did not divide exactly. Demonstrate this to the children:

'We know $4 \div 2 = 2$. It divides exactly and gives a whole number without a remainder. The answer on your calculator is 2 (2.0 on some calculators).'

'We know $10 \div 3 = 3$ remainder 1. It does not divide exactly. The answer on your calculator is 3.333 333 3 which shows that the answer is not just a whole number.'

A game to play

Place number cards face downwards on the table. The first player turns one card over and states whether it will divide exactly by 2, 3, 4, 5. This is then checked by the other player using a calculator. One point is scored for each correct answer; for example, three points are scored for stating 12 will divide by 2, 3 and 4. One point is given to the opponent if the player gives an incorrect answer; for example, stating that 12 will divide by 5. The first player to score a given number of points is the winner.

The numbers on the cards can be chosen according to the children playing. You might also want to simplify the rules.

LINKS WITH THE ENVIRONMENT

Talk about how children share and group in everyday life at home and at school:

- They are often put in groups to play team games, e.g. five-a-side.
- They share cards out equally for board games.
- They may walk in twos or threes in school.
- They sometimes share sweets, money, or belongings with friends or brothers and sisters.

NOTES ON INVESTIGATIONS

Section A

Do the children appreciate the concept of sharing equally? This investigation gives a good opportunity to develop the link between multiplication and division:

12 shared between 3 gives 4   because   3 groups of 4 make 12
$12 \div 3 = 4$ $3 \times 4 = 12$

Section B

Do the children appreciate the relationship between the three numbers – that three numbers allow us to write down four number sentences?

$$3 \times 4 = 12 \qquad\qquad 12 \div 3 = 4$$
$$4 \times 3 = 12 \qquad\qquad 12 \div 4 = 3$$

Talk about this link between multiplication and division: if 12 shared between 3 gives 4, then 3 groups of 4 give 12.

$$12 \div 3 = 4$$

⊙ ⊙ ⊙

$$3 \times 4 = 12$$

You can encourage the children to make up more of their own to do.

Section C

Do the children appreciate the full range of possibilities? Do they adopt a system? For example, do they exhaust all the possibilities using the addition sign first?

Do they make use of the commutative property? Do they make use of the link between multiplication and division?

You may want to introduce a time limit for children to work to, or say that the answers must be 12 or less.

Data 1

Purpose

- To introduce the use and purpose of graphs
- To introduce tallying and the collecting of data
- To introduce block graphs and 1 : 1 scale
- To interpret graphs to obtain information

Materials

Squared paper

Vocabulary

Graph, picture graph, block graph, tally, tallying, squared paper, more, most, fewer, altogether, title, label, least, different

TEACHING POINTS

1 Tallying

Introduce the topic by telling the children how tallying has been used throughout history as a means of counting possessions. Think of situations when it could have been used. Show tallying on the board, e.g. counting animals, days, scores.

Use scores in games lessons, class quizzes and competitions for practice in tallying. Group or team scores are better in order to avoid embarassment to individuals with low scores.

2 Tables

Tally the eye colours of the children in the class and show how to make a table.

Eye colour	green	grey	blue	brown
Number of children	1	2	1	4

Use other data relevant to the children to practise tallying and making tables; e.g. hair colour, colours worn, shoe size.

3 Graphs

Explain that a graph is a picture that shows information. Do class picture graphs of eye colours, either on the board or on large squared paper. Talk about the 'title' and the naming and numbering of the vertical axis. Children will find this easier to understand if the information is about themselves. Talk about other examples of picture graphs.

Use the same data to introduce block graphs. The children can see that picture graphs and block graphs often use the same information.

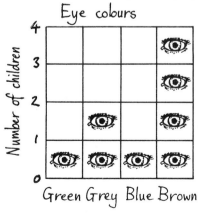

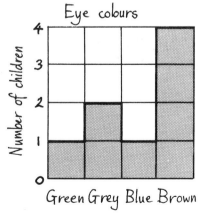

Some children may need extra practice with block graphs as they are a more abstract form of recording.

Can the children think of occasions when the information is more suited to a block graph than to a picture graph (e.g. pocket money)? Discuss which shows the information most clearly or appropriately.

4 Relevance

Graphs do not naturally come into children's daily lives. Although situations will not be entirely realistic, ask the children to suggest information that can be made into graphs. Talk with them about the best type of graph to use and why.

5 Interpretation

The interpretation of graphs is important. Encourage discussion of graphs the children have made. Ask questions about them to show how they give information. Put in some open-ended questions:
'Why don't we all wear shoes of the same size?'
'Why are some children's feet bigger than others?'
These questions will encourage children to reflect and make deductions.

LINKS WITH THE ENVIRONMENT

Links with the world outside school are not always appropriate at this stage as graphs in newspapers, hospitals, etc., tend to use unfamiliar scales or are straight-line graphs.

You can talk about wider uses in the school. These might include class sizes, favourite school dinners, birds visiting the playground or bird table, a census of passing traffic, favourite books, or visitors to school.

NOTES ON INVESTIGATIONS

Section A

Do the children make appropriate choices of data? Extend the work by asking the children to choose situations with a limited number of options that would allow the drawing of simple graphs: for example, colours of jumpers, number of left- or right-handed children, etc.

Section B

Do the children do the tallying correctly? Do they need help in drawing the graph? Do they label and title the graph?

Section C

This is an investigation in interpretation. There are a number of possibilities and the only 'fixed' information is that Laura has 2 more than Mark. Do the children realise this?

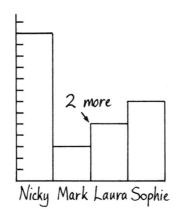 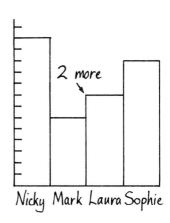

Money 1

Purpose

- To recognise all coins to £1
- To change amounts of money into coins of equal value
- To make up given amounts of money

Materials

Coins (plastic and real)

Vocabulary

Names of coins, pence, money, smallest number, amount, equals, equally, value, share equally, change

TEACHING POINTS

1 Barter

A good start to money is through barter. Children barter over lots of items; for example,

> 5 stickers for one sweet
> 2 marbles for a 'go on your skates'

Encourage the children to talk about other bartering situations.

2 Money

Encourage the children to think about money by talking about trading.
'Can you barter for crisps in a shop?'
'Can you barter for a comic?'

It can be great fun setting up a class shop without using money. At first don't have any 'currency', then have 'pretend money' using bricks, cubes or some other items. Bring the children round to using money and fixing prices for goods. You can use this as role play for class discussion.

When the children want to use coins, introduce them to the different values. Many children will be familiar with these. But play games putting coins in order of value using two, three, four or more coins depending on the children's skills.

Ask the children to find the total value of two coins, three coins, four coins.

Games to play

Use this type of question: 'I have three coins in my hand. One is silver. They make 9p. What are they?' (5p, 2p, 2p)

You can make a card game for matching. Play Snap, Pairs or Dominoes with these.

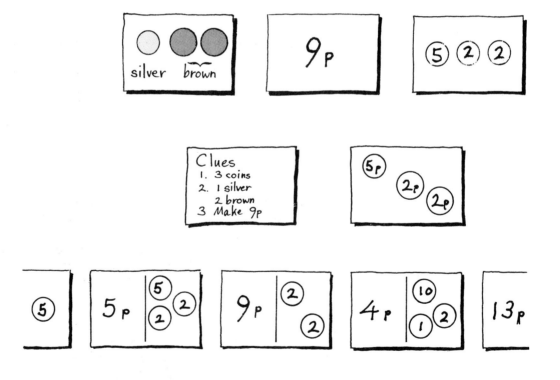

3 Changing coins

Changing coins for others of the same value is sometimes surprisingly difficult. Start with the smaller value coins. Use plastic coins, asking children to change 5p, 10p, 15p, etc. into coins adding up to the same values.

Games to play

DOMINOES

 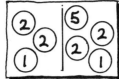 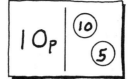 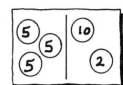

ODD ONE OUT

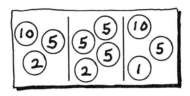 

Use a blank card
to cover up the
'odd amount'.

MENTAL WORK   Draw sets of coins on the board for the children to add up in their
heads.

Ask the children to make an amount of money using a given
number of coins. For example, make 20p using 4 coins.

Ask the children to work out the smallest number of coins they can
carry in their pocket to make up particular amounts; for example, 9p
requires 3 coins.

A game to play

You will need to make some 'pockets' from card or material, and a pile
of 'amount' cards to show the amounts of money to be made.

Each player takes a 'pocket'.

The 'amount' cards are shuffled and placed face down. Players take
a card and make up the smallest number of coins for the amount on
that card. The coins and the card are put in the pocket.

A referee can check the results with a 'checkcard'. One point is
given for a correct answer.

The first to score 5 points is the winner.

Adapt the amounts and points to suit the players.

USING THE
CALCULATOR

Show the children how they can enter amounts of money just as they can enter numbers.

Practise simple addition of pence up to 20p. For example,

7p + 5p

| 7 | + | 5 | = |

Talk about patterns made by addition of coins of equal value. For example,

1(p)	2	3	4	5
2(p)	4	6	8	10
5(p)	10	15	20	25

A game to play

Choose a small amount of money, e.g. 8p. The first player has to make up the amount, entering coin values only, e.g. 5 + 2 + 1.

These can be recorded and checked by a third player – the 'referee'.

The winner is the player who does not repeat a combination or who does not enter a number that is not a coin value, e.g. 3. Different orders of the same coins count as different answers.

Have coins available for checking.

LINKS WITH THE
ENVIRONMENT

- Talk with the children about how we can save money.
- Where do parents use money each day? Garage, telephone, shop, etc.
- Where do children use money?
- What money do they bring to school? Clubs, dinner money, school shop, etc.
- Where does money come from? For example, bank, Royal Mint.

NOTES ON
INVESTIGATIONS

Section A

Are the children systematic? Do they find one way of making 20p, and then change one coin into others? Do they look for more coins of this value?

Section B

Do the children use a logical system? Do they go through the values in order, starting with 1p?

1p → not possible   3p → not possible
2p → ②   4p → ②②

This investigation can be extended by looking at other pairs of coins.

Section C

How is the investigation approached? Do, for example, children first check if the amounts can be made using the same value of coins, e.g. 50p + 50p, before going on to look for combinations?

Number 5

Purpose

To introduce $\frac{1}{2}$ and $\frac{1}{4}$

Materials

Scissors, rectangles, squares, circles, squared paper, gummed paper squares, glue, paper

Vocabulary

Half, halves, quarter, equal, circle, fraction, rectangle, squares, shape, sizes, pattern, divide, dividing

TEACHING POINTS   **1 Half**

The children will know the word 'half' – talk about where they have heard it; for example, half-time, half-hour. (Do they know what these mean?) Think of other examples, like half-way through the lesson, half-way through a book, etc.

Help the children to understand that half means two equal parts.

Using real objects, show that something can be shared into two equal parts. Cake, oranges, plasticine spheres or cylinders all show this clearly. Let the children try cutting objects in half so they get equal parts.

orange   cake   cylinder   sphere

$\dfrac{1}{2}$	$\dfrac{1}{2}$

Emphasise that an object is a 'whole'. When split into two equal parts, each part is one half.

Continue practical work with paper rectangles. Use different sizes and colours. Let the children practise writing $\frac{1}{2}$.

Reinforce the idea of halves with questions.
'Can you match the two parts?'
'What is each part?'
'How many halves make a whole?'

2 Quarter

The word 'quarter' may not be so familiar – but ask where the children
have heard it; for example, quarter-final, quarter past, quarter to.
    Go through practical activities for quarters as you did with halves.

orange   cake   plasticine   paper strip

Point out how the fraction is written: $\frac{1}{4}$. Talk with the children about
what the symbols mean.

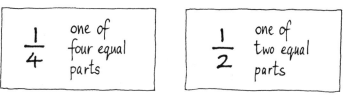

3 Practice

Use circles and squares to show that there are different ways of
dividing in halves or quarters.

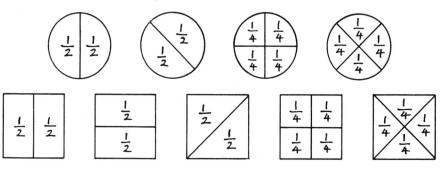

Use string for the children to find out how to divide a length in
halves and quarters.

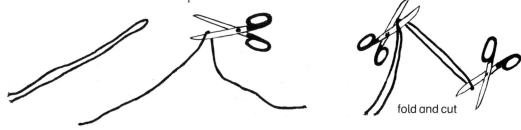

fold and cut

Look for objects in the classroom to divide into halves and quarters for example, display boards, windows, doors, table tops.

 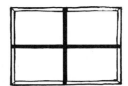 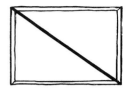

LINKS WITH THE ENVIRONMENT

- Discuss the use of halves and quarters in everyday situations.
- We use 'half' and 'quarter' at meal times – $\frac{1}{2}$ cake, $\frac{1}{4}$ pie, $\frac{1}{2}$ full, $\frac{1}{2}$ slice of bread.
- We use 'half' and 'quarter' in telling the time – $\frac{1}{2}$ past, $\frac{1}{4}$ past/to
- In some games we refer to halves and quarters – half-time, own half, first quarter.
- When travelling we sometimes say we are 'half-way there' or 'a quarter of the way there'.

NOTES ON INVESTIGATIONS

Section A

It is a good idea to have some pre-cut gummed squares of various sizes. Do the children investigate more than one way of folding the card in half? Do they really try to use a variety of square sizes? Do they find different ways of cutting the squares into halves and quarters.

Do they try to be accurate in their folding and cutting (i.e. make sure that the parts are really halves)? Do they still link the halves and quarters when making the pattern?

Section B

Do the children start by folding into halves and quarters? Do any of the children involve counting in their attempts?

Section C

Do the children think ahead and plan shapes that will readily divide into halves and quarters? Do they use the squared paper to 'balance' their shapes? Or do they draw arbitrary shapes and then try to divide them into halves and quarters? Do they draw any shapes that they can only divide into halves?

Length 1

Purpose

- To revise or introduce measuring using arbitrary units
- To revise or introduce appropriate language
- To revise or introduce the units of digit, span, cubit, stride

Materials

Pencil, book, ruler, newspaper

Vocabulary

Comparative language: tall, taller, tallest; short, shorter, shortest; high, higher, highest; low, lower, lowest; long, longer, longest. Digit, span, cubit, stride, measure, height, length, reach, wide, narrow, thick, thin, shallow, deep, long, estimate.

TEACHING POINTS

1 Vocabulary

Begin the topic by using the vocabulary. Relate it all to the children and the classroom.
'Who is the tallest child?'
'Which is higher, the table or the cupboard? Which is the lower?'
'Which is wider, the classroom or the corridor?'

When do the children use 'length' words? There are some lovely art and craft ideas here. Ask them to draw pictures to illustrate these situations: a narrow path, a wide motorway, a long neck – they don't all have to be serious! You can also draw pictures to illustrate pairs of comparative words, e.g. taller and shorter.

Cut pictures out of magazines and newspapers. Make a scrapbook with the pictures, having pages for each word, e.g. low, wide, high, etc.

2 Digit

digit

Talk about how people used to measure and how they used parts of the body as measuring units. The digit was a unit for measuring short distances.
Let the children measure with their digits.

Play guessing games such as estimating the lengths of objects in the classroom in digits (e.g. the length of a desk) and then checking them. Different children may obtain different results. Why is this so?

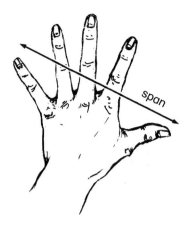

3 Span

Let the children draw round their outstretched hands to show the 'span line' from the tip of the little finger to the tip of the thumb.

Longer objects can be measured in spans. Ask why it is better to use a span rather than a digit for longer objects.

4 Cubit

The cubit is the basic unit on which the pyramids were built. Show that it was from the tip of the longest finger to the elbow.

Let the children measure in cubits and compare their results. Why are they sometimes different?

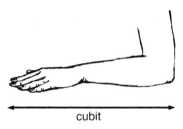

cubit

5 Stride

Show the stride as a long step. Compare strides in the classroom or playground.

Place cut-out footprints on the classroom floor to show the relative strides of some of the children.

LINKS WITH THE ENVIRONMENT

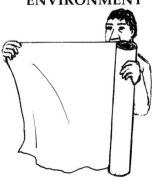

Use appropriate language in the PE lesson.
'Climb higher/lower on the ropes/bars.'
'Bounce balls higher/lower.'
'make short jumps, then long jumps around the hall.'

In art, children can make 'span patterns' using finger paints or by drawing round and painting spans.

Talk about the way in which people used to measure. The pyramids were built using the cubit as the measuring unit. The Romans used a 'pace' to measure roads – this was a double step as they marched (from the heel of a foot to the point where the same heel comes down again). Material was measured from the nose to the end of the outstretched arm.

NOTES ON INVESTIGATIONS

Section A

Is the child's choice of units appropriate? Are the children aware that a larger unit is normally used for a longer distance?

Section B

Do the children approach this in a logical manner? Do they choose both tall and short friends? Do they place their friends in order of height? Do they realise they are looking for a relationship between height and reach? Do they devise a system for comparing both heights and reaches?

Reach	Height
John	John
Brian	Brian
Carol	Carol

Note: In general, height and reach are likely to be related but there may be exceptions to this.

Section C

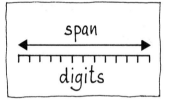

Do the children think of ways to compare these measurements? Do they mark the longer measurement (e.g. the span) before comparing it with the smaller one (e.g. the digit)? Do the children compare their measurements with those of a friend and discover that, in general, our bodies are similar in proportions (e.g. just over 2 spans measure a cubit)?

Weight 1

Purpose

- To revise or introduce vocabulary for weight
- To revise or introduce balancing using arbitrary weights

Materials

Feather, cup, chalk, box, scissors, scales, tin, stone, ruler, plasticine, spoon, cubes (at least 20), pencil, book

Vocabulary

Comparative language: heavy/light, heavier/lighter, heaviest/lightest. Weight, balance, small, large, estimate, scales, balance scales, cube, divide, order, equal, measure

TEACHING POINTS

1 Using weight

Talk with the children about weight.
'What is weight?'
'How do we measure it?' – scales, balances
'Where do we see people measuring the weight of objects?' –
supermarket, sweet shops, market, greengrocer

2 Vocabulary of weight

Ask children to lift objects by hand and compare them: e.g. book,
chalk; brick, cup.
   Ask them to describe the objects using the correct mathematical
vocabulary.
'The brick is heavier than the cup.'
'The cup is lighter than the brick.'
Remind them that 'light' used in this sense does not mean sunlight or
electric light.
   Use three or more objects and compare them.

3 Estimation

Ask the children to estimate which of two objects is heavier. Then
compare by lifting.
   Choose two different objects, the smaller of which is the heavier,
e.g. a polystyrene block and a small heavier box.
   Use two similar boxes or tins, one of which is heavier.
   These activities are to make children aware that we cannot tell the
weight of objects just by looking.

4 Scales

Ask the children to compare the weight of objects, e.g. a tin and a box,
by using the balance scales. Talk about what effect the heavier object
has on the balance scales, i.e. it goes down. What happens to the
lighter object? When will neither side go up or down?

5 Arbitrary units

Ask the children to balance an object like a lump of plasticine, with
cubes and marbles. They can record the results visually at first, and
then go on to written recording:
'The plasticine balances 6 marbles or 7 cubes.'

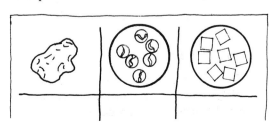

LINKS WITH THE ENVIRONMENT

Think about other times where we see weighing situations.
- The see-saw in the park provides a good practical example of a balance
- On the market – weighing fruit and vegetables
- At the butcher's shop – weighing meat
- At the sweet shop – weighing sweets (pick and mix)
- At home – weighing ingredients for baking
- At the bank – weighing large amounts of coins for exchange into notes

NOTES ON INVESTIGATIONS

Section A

Do the children appreciate that small objects can be heavy and large objects light? Are the children's choices of heavy and light things in comparison to themselves or in comparison to something else (e.g. a book)? Talk about their choice of object as a base for comparison of weight.

Section B

Do the children realise that changing the shape of the plasticine does not change its weight? Discuss this conservation of weight activity with the children.

Section C

How do the children divide the plasticine into two equal pieces – by estimating, or by rolling into a sausage, or by measuring against a ruler? Do they repeat their method in order to divide it into four equal pieces? How do they divide the plasticine into three equal pieces – by trial and error, or by measuring against a ruler?

Volume and capacity 1

Purpose

- To give children experience of filling containers
- To establish the use of the cube as a unit for measuring volume
- To revise the language of capacity
- To give experience of pouring activities
- To revise or introduce arbitrary units of capacity

Materials

Pairs of red and yellow boxes of different sizes, cotton reels, cubes, beakers, paint pots, margarine tubs, jug, yogurt pot, egg cup, plastic bottle, funnel, selection of containers, felt-tipped pen, plasticine, water. (Make sure you have sufficient reels and cubes to fill the red and yellow boxes. It will be easier if the same colour boxes are the same size.)

Vocabulary

Fill, pour, volume, measure, measuring, cube, water level, cuboid, shape, capacity, container, empty, holds more

TEACHING POINTS

1 Volume

This type of question is a good start to discussing volume.
'Why do we have boxes?'
'What are boxes made of?'
'Are all boxes the same shape?' 'What do we buy in boxes?'
'How do we know when a box is full?'
'What does "full" mean?'

Look at a collection of boxes of various sizes and shapes. Talk about the amount of space inside a box being its volume, which can be measured by counting the number of cubes that the box will hold. Use other objects to fill the box. See which objects are better than others. Do the children understand why cubes are useful units to use when measuring volume, as compared to, say, marbles or shells?

Set up practical activities to give children practice in filling a box with different objects. Recording is not important, as long as they begin to appreciate the concept of 'volume'.

Set up an estimating activity. Have several boxes and ask the children to estimate how many cubes each will hold, and to place the boxes in order of volume. Let them check by filling the boxes with cubes. This is a useful group activity.

Ask the children to make shapes with building blocks. Show that the amount of space they take up is found by counting the number of bricks.

2 Capacity

Can the children describe a liquid? What liquids do they like? Which ones can they drink? Which liquids are useful?
'What are liquids?'
'What sort of containers hold liquids?'
'Are they all the same shape and size?'
'Do they all hold the same amount of liquid?'
'How can we measure the amount of liquid we put in a container?' –

We can use egg cups, paint pots, beakers, yogurt pots, tins, spoons.

Ask the children to suggest a measure for filling a jam-jar, and another for filling the sink.

'Why would we use different measures for these?'

Collect different containers or pictures of different sized and shaped bottles. These can make an interesting display.

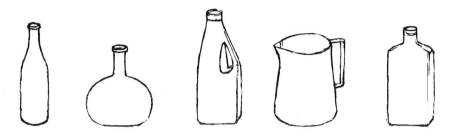

Ask a volunteer to choose a suitable measure for filling a given container. Why was it chosen? Was it the best choice? Would other children choose the same or a different one? Ask the children to estimate how many times the measure will have to be filled in order to fill the container. Ask someone to fill the container and see if the class are correct.

Let the children practise estimating capacity and putting containers in order. Get them to check if their estimates are correct.

Find three bottles of different shapes but the same capacity. First get the children to estimate their capacities in order. Then, using a suitable measure, see what the bottles hold. Shape can be deceptive – do the children understand this?

Ask two children to fill identical lemonade bottles with identical measures, e.g. egg cups. Do they get the same answer every time? They should, of course, but does this work out in practice? How can they be more accurate with filling?

LINKS WITH THE ENVIRONMENT

If possible make a trip to a supermarket or shop to look at different shaped and sized containers. Ask the children to bring in empty containers, or see how many different things they can find at home. Which ones are suitable for filling with liquid or cubes?

In the home, what containers do we have for holding water or liquids? – Bath, sink, kettle, fish bowl, watering can, drink container in a lunch box

What containers do we have for solids? – Biscuit tins, Oxo boxes, bathcube boxes

NOTES ON INVESTIGATIONS

Section A

Do the children appear to have a realistic view of the capacity of a bucket, a bottle and a jug? Do they choose realistic containers to be measured with these?

Section B

Do the children appreciate the shape of a cuboid? Do they appreciate that they could increase the height of the cuboid as well as the width?
    Possible answers are:
$8 \times 1 \times 1$, $2 \times 2 \times 2$, $4 \times 2 \times 1$
They all have a volume of 8 cubes.
    As an extension, other shapes can be made from 8 cubes, or use 12 cubes.

Section C

This activity leads to the conservation of volume. Do the children realise that the water level remains the same each time? Discuss the reason for this, i.e. that despite the change of shape the plasticine displaces the same amount of water each time.

Purpose

To revise the days of the week and months of the year

Materials

Squared paper, local newspaper, card, paper

Vocabulary

Today, tomorrow, yesterday, days, week, months, year, days of the week, months of the year, calendar, first, last, order, summer, winter, before, after

TEACHING POINTS

1 Days of the week

Teach the children rhymes which go through the days of the week.
'Sneeze on Monday, sneeze for danger'
'Solomon Grundy'
'Monday's child is fair of face'
The wolf's rhyme from *Polly and Stupid Wolf* by Catherine Storr (Puffin, p.47)

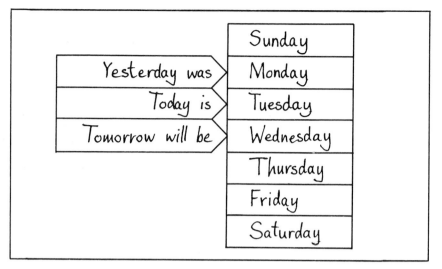

Use visual aids; this chart is simple to make.

Play 'Questions and answers' using the chart.

'What day is it today?'

'What day will it be tomorrow?'

'What day was it yesterday?'

'How many days are there in one week?'

'What day will it be one week from today?'

'What are the days of the week?'

Score points for correct answers in teams (practise grouping) and tally the points.

2 Months of the year

The children may not be aware of the sequence of months.

Relate the order of the months to a wheel. This will help children to understand the cycle of months. Make a visual aid where the 'months wheel' can turn to match the pointers.

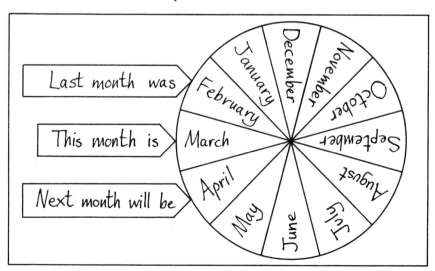

3 Practice

Keep a class diary for a few weeks. This is less demanding than individual ones, but still reinforces sequencing.

A simple weather chart is interesting for a short period of time, especially if you have some dramatic weather during it.

Make some games to give practice in sequencing.

Games to play

FISHING GAME

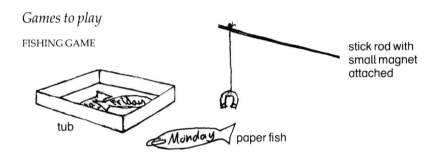

stick rod with small magnet attached

tub

Monday paper fish

You need a tub containing paper fish. Each fish has one day or month written on it and a paper clip attached. You also need a stick rod with a small magnet attached.

A group of children 'fish' for the days of the week. The starting point does not matter, as long as the sequence of 'fishing' is correct.

CAN YOU GO?

You need lots of cards with the days or months written on. (Blank playing cards produced by E.J. Arnold are useful for making card games quickly.)

Give each player an equal number of cards. One person puts down a card. The next person must put down a card with the following day/ month etc. If they cannot go they pick up a card from another pile if there are sufficient cards.

MENTAL WORK   Ask the children questions about days and months.
'How many days are in 1 week, 2 weeks, 3 weeks?'
'If today is Monday 17th, what date will it be next Monday?'
Ask questions involving yesterday, today and tomorrow.
'What is the 5th month of the year?'
'What number is your birthday month?'
'How many months are in 1 year, 2 years?'

USING THE CALCULATOR

'How many days are in three weeks?'

$\boxed{3}\ \boxed{\times}\ \boxed{7}\ \boxed{=}$

$\boxed{7}\ \boxed{+}\ \boxed{7}\ \boxed{+}\ \boxed{7}\ \boxed{=}$

'How many weeks are in 28 days?'

$\boxed{2}\ \boxed{8}\ \boxed{\div}\ \boxed{7}\ \boxed{=}$

$\boxed{2}\ \boxed{8}\ \boxed{-}\ \boxed{7}\ \boxed{=}\ \boxed{-}\ \boxed{7}\ \boxed{=}\ \boxed{-}\ \boxed{7}\ \boxed{=}\ \boxed{-}\ \boxed{7}\ \boxed{=}\ \boxed{0}$

These activities may be done using $+$, $-$, $\times$, $\div$ and the constant function.

LINKS WITH THE ENVIRONMENT

Discuss the happenings during the week. These might include schooldays, weekends, days for shopping or sport.

Do children have favourite days? Why?

Where do we find calendars? When do we use them?

NOTES ON INVESTIGATIONS

Section A

You will need to have several copies of the local newspaper (free or otherwise) available. The children may need help in finding the right pages. Are the children competent in looking up the information? Do they realise that information of this type usually appears in the same place in the paper each time?

Section B

Are the children's answers sensible and appropriate? Can the children explain their reasoning for their choice of months and events?

Section C

Do the children appreciate that the months of the year go in a cycle? Are they competent in looking up information for years that start with a month other than January?

Angles 1

Purpose

To introduce or revise left and right turns

Materials

Squared paper, plain paper

Vocabulary

Right, left, turn, forward

TEACHING POINTS

1 Looking right and left

Talk with the children about turning left and right.
'What do you see if you look to your right?'
'What do you see if you look to your left?'
  Talk with the children about right and left parts of the body – hand, foot, eye, ear, etc.

2 Turning right and left

Show some road signs like these. Look in the Highway Code or some road safety literature.
'What direction do these signs tell us to go?'

3 Directions

'If you go through the classroom door and want to go to the (. . . hall . . .), which way do you turn?'

A game to play

One child closes their eyes or is blindfolded and follows directions around the classroom. Use only the directions 'right', 'left' and 'forward'.

4 Other orientations

Ask the children:
'Which is my right hand?'
'Which is my left foot?'
'What do I see if I turn to my right?'
'Who is on my left?'
   Do this again with children taking your place.

A game to play

Have three children sitting facing the class. The middle child asks:
'Who is on my left?'
'Who is on my right?'
   This can also be done with four children, taking turns to ask questions.

LINKS WITH THE ENVIRONMENT   Talk with the children about things they see turning left. And what they see on the left or right.

   • On the road – cars, bicycles; road signs
   • On the way to school – people turning; shops to the left; road on the right

NOTES ON INVESTIGATIONS

Section A

Do the children record the directions correctly as they make the words?

Section B

Do the children find the orientation difficult? Do they understand the notation, R2 etc.? Are they able to find other ways of scoring goals?

Section C

This is an exercise in orientation. Do the children make the transition from their own right and left to the right and left of another person? Do the children's sentences match up correctly with the faces?

   This investigation could be extended to include more faces.

Number 6

Purpose

- To illustrate the technique of bridging tens on the number line
- To teach the exchange or 'carrying' process for addition of tens and units using structural apparatus
- To extend place value to hundreds, tens and units

Materials

100 square, structural apparatus, calculator, counters, squared paper

Vocabulary

Counters, answers, sums, square, order, numbers, hundreds, tens, units, larger, largest, smallest, triangle, shape, add, altogether, 100 square

TEACHING POINTS

1 Patterns

Start the topic with questions to increase children's awareness of pattern in number. Look at a 100 square.
'What happens when we reach the number 10?' – We start with the 1 again (the 1 in 11).
'What happens when we reach the number 20?
   Use a number board or 100 square. Ask the children if they can predict patterns.
'Look at the numbers ending in 9, e.g. 9, 19, 29 . . . Add on 3 each time. What pattern have you got now?'
   Show these on the number board or 100 square. Ask the children to predict the pattern.

2 Bridging the tens

Demonstrate the pattern that is formed when the tens are 'bridged' on the number line. Make a 'bridge' to show patterns. This one is for + 3, but others can be made, e.g. + 5, + 6.

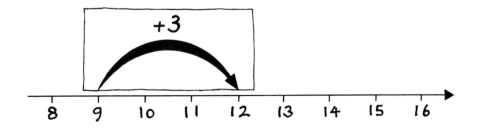

3 Addition with exchange or 'carrying' from the units

Use structural apparatus to show exchange or 'carrying' from the units in addition. Keep to your usual form of words and method for teaching and recording this. The important point here is to encourage children to develop some imagery, rather than just manipulating the apparatus and numbers. Lots of practice and reinforcement with the apparatus helps children to develop the imagery.

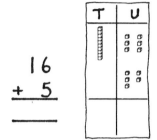
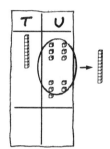
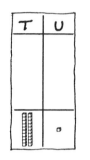

4 Hundreds, tens and units

Begin place value to HTU, using structural apparatus like Unifix, Centicube or Dienes apparatus.

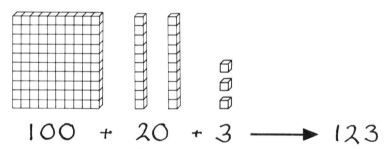

$$100 \quad + \quad 20 \quad + \quad 3 \longrightarrow 123$$

Use number cards to reinforce place value. These can be put on top of each other to make up numbers.

$$\boxed{1 \mid 0 \mid 0} + \boxed{2 \mid 0} + \boxed{3} \longrightarrow \boxed{1 \mid 2 \mid 3}$$

Ask children to give the value of individual numbers like the 3 in 347 or the 2 in 123.

Practise oral counting round a group. When a bell rings (or some other sound), the last one to say a number writes it down. Watch that 110 doesn't become 1010!

Games to play

GRAB

Make up packs of number cards – some hundreds, some tens and some units.

Children play in threes, having one type of card each. They make up a number with these cards, and the first one to call it out 'grabs' the 'trick'. This is good oral practice, although it might be noisy!

ORDERS

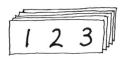

Make up a pack of HTU numbers. Share the cards into sets of three. Each set must be ordered smallest to largest.

This can be played as a game with a group, or individually.

MENTAL WORK   Ask the children the next number in a pattern, e.g. 39, 49, 59, . . .
Write the next number after 109, 1 less than 100, etc.
Add 10 to numbers.
Show the children the quick way of adding 9, i.e. $+10-1$

USING THE CALCULATOR   Revise with the children how to switch on the calculator and enter two- and three-digit numbers.
Let the children practise sums, e.g. $6 + 17 + 29$.

A game to play

Two players use one calculator.
The first player writes down two three-digit numbers which differ by one digit: for example,
147 and 347   or   284 and 294   or   365 and 368
The other player has to make one number into the other by adding only one number. The players then change over.
The first to score ten correct answers is the winner.

LINKS WITH THE ENVIRONMENT   Get the children to spot numbers greater than 100 on their way to school or in school. These might include the number of children in school, the numbers on houses, car numbers. (Do all cars have three-digit numbers?)
What do 100 pencils look like? What about 100 books? Show what 100 'things' look like from the stockroom.
Build up displays of 100, 200, 300, etc., using grains of rice or other small objects.

If you can, point out to children how many children are in the hall, etc., at particular times (assembly, school plays). If your school is not large enough, choose another large gathering of children or people.

NOTES ON INVESTIGATIONS

Section A

Do the children have a system in finding the numbers 122, 125, 126, 152, etc.? Are they able to write them in order? Do they appreciate they group them in order of hundreds first, then tens, then in order of the units?

Section B

Do the children find it easy to identify the value of the 3? Do they realise how to make a number that can go into two sacks (i.e. there must be two 3s in the number)? Do they realise how to make a number that can go into all three sacks (i.e. there must be three 3s–333)?

Section C

How do the children approach this investigation? Do they complete one line before moving on to the next? Do they appreciate that the 'key' numbers are the corner ones?

This investigation can be extended to other totals. For example, the numbers 1, 2, 3, 4, 5, 6 can also be used to make a total of 10, 11 or 12.

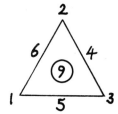 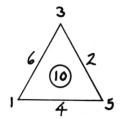 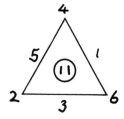 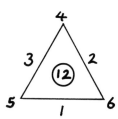

Do the children realise that the larger totals require the larger numbers at the corners?

Number 7

Purpose

- To revise subtraction number bonds
- To introduce subtraction of tens and units using the method of decomposition
- To extend place value to hundreds, tens and units

Materials

Abacus, number cards to demonstrate place value, structural apparatus, squared paper, calculator

Vocabulary

Take away, subtract, difference between, less than, fewer than, abacus, number sentence, smallest, largest, order

TEACHING POINTS

1 Patterns

Show patterns in number by counting down.
'Count down in ones from 20.' – 20, 19, 18, 17, . . .
'What happens when we reach 10?' – We get 10, 9, 8, 7, . . .
'Can you see a pattern?'
'Count down from 30 to 20 in ones. Do we get the same pattern?' – 29, 28, 27, . . . , 19, 18, 17, . . . , 9, 8, 7, . . .

  Show the pattern when the tens are 'bridged' on the number line.
Make 'bridges' (as in Number 6) to show subtraction numbers.

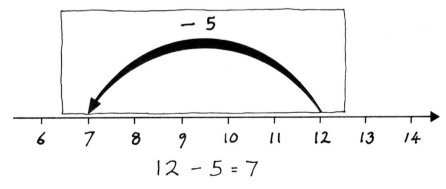

Show how subtraction can form patterns.
$$12 - 5 = 7$$
$$22 - 5 = 17$$
$$32 - 5 = 27$$
$$42 - 5 = 37$$

2 Decomposition

The method of decomposition will need a lot of practical work.
Practise changing a ten to ten units.

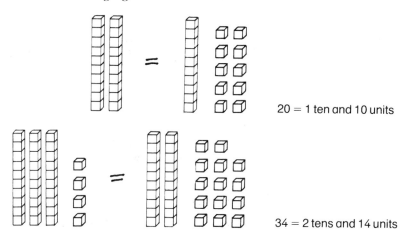

20 = 1 ten and 10 units

34 = 2 tens and 14 units

When children are happy decomposing a ten, start to do
subtractions.

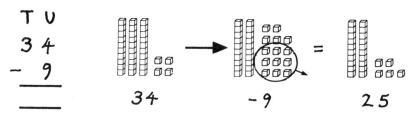

As soon as the children understand what is happening you can
show the recording. For example,

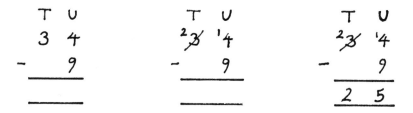

Use your normal language and phrasing to explain the processes to
the children. Keep it enjoyable by bringing in humour.
    Take time developing the imagery. It is important for children to
understand what they are doing, so don't rush it.

A game to play

SHAKEDOWN

This game gives excellent practice in decomposition. Children can
play it individually or in groups.

Each player needs a place-value board. Also needed is a pile of cards showing TU numbers, a shaker and a dice, plus some structural apparatus.

   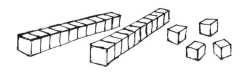 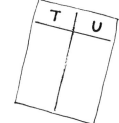

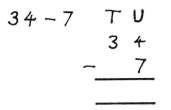 Each player takes a card and puts out apparatus on their board to show the number. Children take turns to shake the dice and take off the number shown on the dice.
They keep going until all the cubes are taken off.

3 Recording

Practise moving from the horizontal to the vertical.

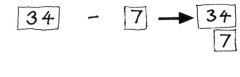

$$34 - 7$$

$$\begin{array}{r} T\ U \\ 3\ 4 \\ -\ \ 7 \\ \hline \\ \hline \end{array}$$

4 HTU place value

Show place value to HTU using an abacus.

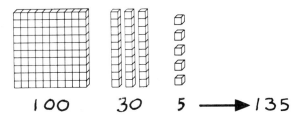

You can also show this by threading beads or reels on string. Reinforce this using structural apparatus.

100   30   5 ⟶ 135

Number cards may also be used.

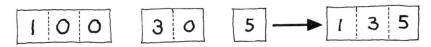

Talk about the values of numbers according to their positions to test understanding.
'What is the value of the 7 in 327?'
'What is the value of the 2?'
'What is the value of the 3?'

MENTAL WORK
Subtract 10 from numbers.
 Discuss the quick way of subtracting 9, i.e. $-10+1$.
 Give the children the words. Let them write the numbers.

USING THE CALCULATOR
Revise with the children how to switch on the calculator and enter two- digit numbers, and how to use the CANCEL button rather than the ON/OFF switch.
 Let the children practise subtraction bonds, e.g. $18-3$.
 Discuss the patterns they get by repeated subtraction, e.g. 20, 18, 16, 14, . . . ; 19, 16, 13, 10, . . .

A game to play

Two players use one calculator. The first player writes down two three-digit numbers which differ by only one digit; for example,
347 and **147**   or   **294** and **284**   or   **365** and **368**
The second player enters the larger number on the calculator and has to make the other number by subtracting only one number:
$347-200=147$

LINKS WITH THE ENVIRONMENT
Where do the children find subtraction patterns in everyday life? These might include: house numbers (32, 30, 28, 26 . . .); the countdown for a spaceship launch or on a kitchen timer (10, 9, 8, 7, . . .); reducing amounts in money displays on payphones; the water-level indicators on lock gates. Some of these might not be familiar to all the children.

NOTES ON INVESTIGATIONS
Section A

There is the opportunity here to consolidate the links between addition and subtraction. When children have chosen two numbers, do they realise the restrictions on choosing the third?

Section B

Do the children look for a constant difference and use all the rungs?

Section C

Writing each number on a piece of paper and then arranging them in order can be helpful.

Purpose

- To revise or introduce the cube, cuboid, cylinder, pyramid, cone, triangular prism and sphere
- To consider the properties of these shapes
- To relate these solid shapes to the environment

Materials

Set of solid shapes, collection of grocery containers, plasticine, paper, plasticine board, ruler, plastic knives, paper

Vocabulary

Face, vertex (plural vertices), edge, cube, cuboid, cylinder, cone, sphere, pyramid, triangular prism, square, triangle, rectangle, half, tallest, shortest

TEACHING POINTS

1 Names

Check that the children are familiar with the names of the solid shapes, and can recognise the words. The amount of time needed will depend upon the children's earlier experience.

Play games for reinforcement.

Games to play

PICK A SHAPE

Put all the shapes in a bag. One child puts a hand in the bag and pulls out a shape. The child who correctly names this shape pulls the next one out of the bag.

MATCH

You need a set of name cards, one for each shape.

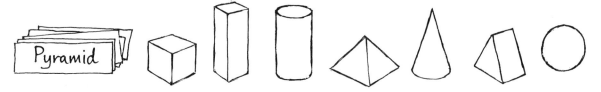

One child sets out the shapes with the name cards randomly arranged beside. Another child must match the shapes to their correct names.

2 Containers

Use containers brought in from home, either packets, boxes, or tins, for children to identify as solid shapes.

Hold up the different containers for children to tell you the names . . . or play the game 'Match' again, but with these containers.

3 Properties

Talk with the children about faces, vertices and edges. Use bricks, boxes, packets, and other containers to make children familiar with the words. They will need to recognise them. Play word games to help with this, using the words. (See the game 'Spot the word' at the end of this teaching point.)

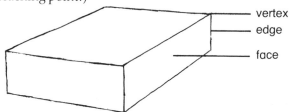

Count the number of faces, vertices and edges of different solid shapes.

Talk about the shapes of the faces.
'A cube has square faces.'
'How are a cube and a cuboid different?'

Talk about which shapes will roll or stack easily. How do shops and supermarkets stack different shaped packages?

Ask children to look at and to describe a shape to a friend (or a group or the class) who has to guess the shape from the description.

Games to play

SPOT THE WORD

Put out counters, one for each letter of the word, e.g. 'edge', 'cuboid', etc. When a child gets a letter correct they write it and collect a counter.

The one with the most counters is the winner.

This game can be played for any words. Adapt it according to your class, and the number of players. Team points can be given instead of counters.

THE YES/NO GAME

Someone puts a shape behind a book, and the other children have to guess what it is. They may ask questions about its properties but only yes or no answers are allowed. For example, 'Are all its faces squares?'

'FEELY' BAG

Put the solid shapes in a 'feely' bag and ask individual children to put their hand in the bag and take out the shape named on a card. The card can be picked from a pile.

USING THE CALCULATOR

The topic of shape doesn't easily lend itself to calculator work, but children can solve number puzzles using the properties of shapes. For example:
'How many edges have 3 cubes? Can you discover at least two ways of finding out, using a calculator?'

$$12 + 12 + 12$$
$$3 \times 12$$

or use the constant function.

LINKS WITH THE ENVIRONMENT

Talk with the children about where we see solid shapes in the environment. For example:
- on the sports field – balls are spheres
- in the shops – boxes and tins etc.
- on the way to school – drainpipes, telephone boxes, gate-posts
- in school – boxes, balls, tables, etc.

NOTES ON INVESTIGATIONS

Section A

Do the children understand the properties of the cuboid and the cylinder? Can they think of a cylinder as a 'flatter' shape and not just a tube or can (for example, 2p coin)?

How many unusual forms of cylinders can they find (for example, pencils, straws)?

Section B

Do the children recognise and name the shapes correctly? Do the children come to realise that many objects like chairs are a combination of the solid shapes introduced? Do they become more aware of the solid shapes which are in the environment?

gap

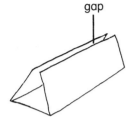

Section C

It is possible to make all of the shapes out of paper by folding and holding the shape in place. Some of the shapes will be 'open'. You may prefer children to use glue for some shapes.

NB It is not intended that 'nets' of solid shapes be introduced at this stage.

Number 8

Purpose

- To use 'counting on' to build up number patterns for multiplication for 2, 3, 4, 5 and 10
- To revise the commutative property

Materials

Squared paper, 100 squares, structural apparatus (e.g. multilink), stop watch or sand timer

Vocabulary

Number, pattern, 100 square, multiplications, rectangles, sets, apparatus, tables, time yourself.

TEACHING POINTS   ### 1 Patterns

Counting on in sets can be done in many different ways.

– Use the calculator to make the pattern of 3. Use either
3 + 3 + 3 + . . . or the constant function.
– Show the pattern of 3 on the number line.

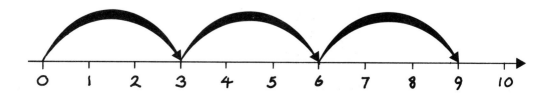

Think of other ways of showing it.

Let children talk and experiment. See how many ways they can find. One way might be:

1   2   (3)   4   5   (6)   7   8   (9)   10   11   (12)

2 Links

Another method that has links with division is to use squared paper:

1	2	3
4	5	6
7	8	9
10	11	12

Children can use this method to show, for example, how many hands five people have. They are showing the links between addition and multiplication.

1	2
3	4
5	6
7	8
9	10

1 person = 2 hands $1 \times 2 = 2$

2 people = 2 + 2 $2 \times 2 = 4$

3 people = 2 + 2 + 2 $3 \times 2 = 6$

4 people = 2 + 2 + 2 + 2 $4 \times 2 = 8$

5 people = 2 + 2 + 2 + 2 + 2 $5 \times 2 = 10$

3 Commutative property

Show the children that multiplication is commutative. This can be done on squared paper.

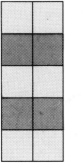

5 sets of 2

5×2

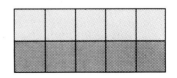

2 sets of 5

2×5

Show the children the multiplication square as far as 5 × 5. This reinforces the commutative property. Pick out some patterns. Then let the children find their own.

×	1	2	3	4	5
1	1	2	3	4	5
2	2	4	6	8	10
3	3	6	9	12	15
4	4	8	12	16	20
5	5	10	15	20	25

Here is one possibility:

```
    2
2   4   6   8   10   The line increases + 2
    6
    8
    10
```

MENTAL WORK   Ask the children to count in 2s, 3s, 4s, 5s and 10s.
Ask children to find the next number in a pattern, e.g.
5 10 15 ☐
Ask the children questions on the commutative property, e.g. 'Write 3 × 2 another way.'
Ask multiplication bonds, e.g. 8 × 5.
See 'Links with the environment'.

A game to play

BUZZ

Decide a pattern of numbers, e.g. 3s. Count round the group (or class), starting at 1. Instead of saying the numbers in the 3s pattern, they say 'Buzz'!
1 2 buzz 4 5 buzz etc.
For the 5s pattern say 'Fizz':
1 2 3 4 fizz 6 7 8 9 fizz etc.
You can have two patterns counted together using fizz-buzz. For example, for 3s and 5s:
1 2 buzz 4 fizz buzz 7 8 buzz etc.

USING THE CALCULATOR

Practise multiplication of single-digit numbers. The children can build up the tables of 3 and 4 both by adding on, and by the use of the constant function.

A game to play

1	2	3	4	5
6	7	8	9	10
11	12	13	14	15

Take a 1–15 rectangle. Use the numbers 1, 2, 3, 4, 5 and the × sign as many times as you like. Cross off the numbers you can make. Which numbers are left?

Make up another game like this.

LINKS WITH THE ENVIRONMENT

sandwiches

Look around the classroom for sets of objects, e.g. four legs on a chair, pairs of children at desks or tables, arms and legs on children.

Play games of mental arithmetic. Add the number of legs on three chairs to the number of arms on two children.

Look at place settings at dinner time – each child has a knife, fork and spoon:
'How many pieces are needed for five children?'

Children often bring sandwiches cut into four.
'How many slices need to be cut for three children?'
'How many individual sandwiches is this?'

Work out the number of sandwiches needed for a family picnic or a party. Use the calculator for this.

NOTES ON INVESTIGATIONS

Section A

Do the children attempt to find a system for detecting the patterns? Do they, for example, write down the numbers in order and look for patterns?

3   4   6   8   9   10   12   15   16   20
10   15   20
4   8   12   16   20
3   6   9   12   15

Do they realise that there are patterns related to the tables of 3 and 4 and 5? Children can, of course, produce other patterns, such as 4, 6, 8, 10, 12.

Section B

Do the children relate the patterns of 3 and 4 to the work they have been doing with the tables of 3 and 4? Do they extend the patterns beyond 10 × 3 and 10 × 4? Do they discover a pattern that allows them to predict which squares to colour rather than count on each time?

Section C

Do the children adopt a system? For example,
2×2
2×3
2×5 etc.
Do they apply the commutative property?

Purpose

To introduce the concept of measuring area by counting squares

Materials

Squared paper, glue

Vocabulary

Squares, area, rectangle

TEACHING POINTS   **1 Counting squares**

Draw some pictures or shapes made from whole squares.

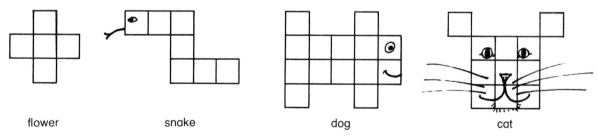

flower   snake   dog   cat

What shapes can children find in the pictures? – squares and
rectangles?
What do they think is the best shape to use to measure the whole
shape? – The answer should be 'square'!
   How many squares are in each shape?

2 Finding area

Do this by counting the number of squares which cover it. Show how
to record the areas: for example,
area of dog = 14 squares

The children can draw their own pictures or patterns on squared paper using whole squares. Show them how to record the area of their pictures and patterns. It is interesting to use squared paper with different sizes of squares, to show that we measure area by counting squares.

Games to play

BOXES

Start off with a 6 × 6 grid of dots. Children take it in turns to join a pair of dots horizontally or vertically. The aim is to make up squares and put in their intitials, by joining a pair of dots. They get another go when they make a square or 'box'. The winner is the one with the biggest area covered by initials.

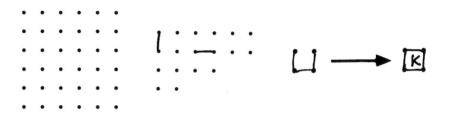

For larger numbers of players, increase the size of the grid.

COVER UP

This is a game for two players. They need a different coloured crayon each, a shaker and a 1–6 dice, plus a 6 × 6 square.

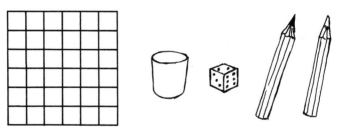

The players take turns to shake the dice. They colour the number of squares shown on the dice. Squares must be edge matched; that is,

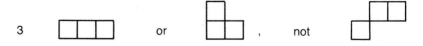

A player who cannot colour in the number of squares shown on the dice, misses their turn. The winner is the player who colours the most squares.

For more players, increase the size of the square.

USING THE CALCULATOR   Draw a picture or shape made from whole squares: for example,

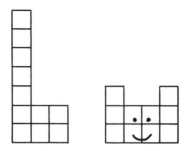

Record the area. Ask the children to use the calculator to find how many squares there would be in 5 pictures (or 4 or 7 . . .). The children can use repeated addition or multiplication or the constant function.

LINKS WITH THE ENVIRONMENT   Talk with the children about where we may see whole squares in the environment.

- In school – some window frames, floor tiles, ceiling tiles, playground drawings, e.g. hopscotch, may be made of whole squares. Ask the children to count the squares and work out the area.
- On the way to school – some pavements, paths, patios, door designs.
- At home – some board games (e.g. snakes and ladders, draughts), some puzzles, and some wallpaper designs are made of whole squares. Pictures or games can be brought into school and displayed with their areas.

NOTES ON INVESTIGATIONS

Section A

Do the children use whole squares for their mosaic patterns? Do they record the areas correctly?

Section B

Are the children systematic in working out how many squares and rectangles are possible?

squares: $1 \times 1, 2 \times 2, 3 \times 3$
rectangles: $1 \times 2, 1 \times 3, 1 \times 4, \ldots , 1 \times 12$
             $2 \times 3, 2 \times 4, 2 \times 5, 2 \times 6$
             3×4

Do they appreciate that some rectangles they can draw are the same, i.e. $1 \times 2 = 2 \times 1$?

Section C

Do the children realise that the next larger square must be 9 squares?
(A 1 × 9 rectangle can also be drawn.)
Do the children appreciate that squares must be linked to the
following number series?

   1   4   9   16   25   36

i.e. 1 × 1   2 × 2   3 × 3   4 × 4   5 × 5   6 × 6

   It is possible to draw several different rectangles for some of the
square numbers. For example.

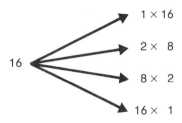

This makes an interesting talking point!
   NB Mathematically speaking, squares are of course rectangles, but
this distinction is not being drawn for children at this stage.

Number 9

Purpose

- To introduce division as repeated subtraction
- To introduce the division sign

Materials

Squared paper, multiplication square

Vocabulary

Number line, sets of, multiplication square, divide, division

TEACHING POINTS

1 The number line

Show how division can be illustrated on the number line by repeated subtraction.

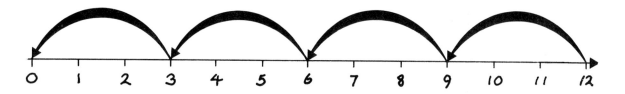

Start at 12. Move back 3 spaces each time. How many 'jumps' does it take to get to zero?

2 Apparatus

The children can practise more repeated subtraction using themselves or counters and taking away 3 each time.

You can also use structural apparatus.

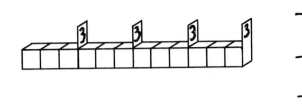

Show ways of recording.

There are 4 sets of 3 in 12.
$12 \div 3 = 4$

You can also show this on the calculator.

3 The multiplication square

Build up a 5 × 5 multiplication square and use it to show the link between division and multiplication.

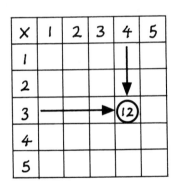

$3 \times 4 = 12$
3 sets of 4 = 12
$12 \div 4 = 3$
How many groups of 4 in 12?

4 Division signs

Introduce the division sign and show how the recording is done:

$$3 \overline{)\, 12}^{\,4} \quad 12 \div 3 = 4$$

NB Although this is often spoken as 'How many 3s are in 12?' it can also be spoken, when appropriate, as '12 shared between 3 gives 4'.

MENTAL WORK   Ask the children division questions in different forms: for example,

12 divided by 3
12 shared by 3
How many 3s are in 12?
12 divided by 3 is 4 because . . .

Ask for number sentences using 3, 4 and 12; for example,

$$3 \times 4 = 12 \quad 12 \div 4 = 3$$

Ask verbal questions such as 'Share 8 marbles between 4 children'.

USING THE CALCULATOR

Show repeated subtraction on the calculator.
'Start at 12. Count how many times 3 is subtracted to get to zero.'

$$\boxed{12}\;\boxed{-}\;\boxed{3}\;\boxed{-}\;\boxed{3}\;\boxed{-}\;\boxed{3}\;\boxed{-}\;\boxed{3}\;\boxed{=}\;\boxed{0}$$

Show how to press $\boxed{-}$ $\boxed{3}$ four times to get to zero.
Explain that if they cannot get exactly to zero then the number does not divide exactly.
The constant function can also be used.
Use this activity to let children see that they can go to numbers less than zero. For example,

−3 is 3 less than zero,
−6 is 6 less than zero.

A game to play

Lay out a number of division sentences face down, for example, 15 ÷ 3. The first player turns over any one card and has to say how many times $\boxed{-}$ $\boxed{3}$ must be pressed to get to zero. A correct answer scores one point. Players take turns to turn over a card. The first player to score a given number of points is the winner.

LINKS WITH THE ENVIRONMENT

Talk with children about how division/subtraction arises in everyday situations. For example:

- Paying off weekly instalments of money. How many weeks do we have to pay for?
- Grouping situations such as groups in PE lessons.

NOTES ON INVESTIGATIONS

Section A

Do the children try a logical approach? Do they start with the largest number? Do they realise that some numbers do not divide exactly by others?
In the second part of the investigation do they work systematically through the tables they know?

Section B

Do the children realise that each row must be the same length, so that the number of bricks in each row must divide exactly into 20?

You can extend this by looking at a different number of bricks.

Section C

Do the children use a logical method to record their results? For example:

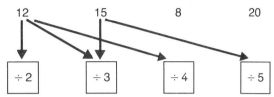

The work can be extended to find other numbers that will fit into three boxes or to find a number that will fit into all four boxes.

Purpose

To find positions on a grid

Materials

Large squared paper, small squared paper

Vocabulary

Square, map, plan, row, column, grid, nearest, code

TEACHING POINTS   **1 Positions on a grid**

Draw a grid for a simple garden plan on the board. Ask the children what they would like you to draw on the plan, such as a pond, a fir tree, a rabbit hutch and a flower bed. Can they tell you which square to put them in?

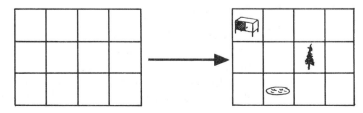

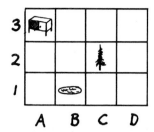

Talk about how we can place objects exactly by counting the squares along and then up.

Use letters and numbers at this stage as it is clearer for the children to see what is happening.

2 Labelling grids

Show the children how to give the letter along the bottom first, and the number up the side second to show the position, so the fir tree is in C2. Let the children think of other items for the garden and tell you their positions.

3 Activities

There are numerous games and activities for using grids; for example, battleships, imaginary islands, and treasure maps.

Ask the children to draw a grid of a treasure island as a class activity and to make a large one for display.

A game to play

Chalk a simple grid on the playground or hall floor. Have two teams. Call out the grid position for one square. Let one child from each team race to it to score a point for their team.

LINKS WITH THE ENVIRONMENT

Use a local street plan and let the children find the position of their home or school.

Look at a local map to pick out familiar buildings and features.

Look at maps their parents might use when travelling.

Play computer games that use grid references, such as chess and battleships.

NOTES ON INVESTIGATIONS

Section A

Do the children draw each of the items in its own square. Do they label the grid correctly? With the letter before the number? You can extend this activity by adding other items and by planning a route around the playground.

Section B

Do the children look for words of different lengths? Do they write the grid positions correctly?

B   U   T   T   E   R   F   L   Y
C3   A1   B3   C1   A2   B2   C2   A3   B1

Extend this activity by letting the children make their own grids and write code words for their friends to decipher.

Section C

Check that the children understand that a row is horizontal and a column is vertical.

Do they try to place one set of animals first and then another? Do they label the rows and columns correctly?

Let them compare answers with their friends.

	A	B	C	D
4	Cow	Sheep		
3		Cow	Sheep	
2			Cow	Sheep
1	Sheep			Cow

Money 2

Purpose

- To revise or introduce the addition of pence with exchange or 'carrying'
- To revise or introduce the cost of buying a number of objects at a given price
- To calculate simple bills
- To find change using the counting on method

Materials

Coins, calculator

Vocabulary

Buy, spend, change, bill, coins, purse, total, smallest

TEACHING POINTS

1 Shopping and change

Talk with the children about when they go shopping. This can be spending pocket money, buying crisps and biscuits at school, or family presents. Ask them how they know the price of the things they buy.

Talk about where they pay and what happens if they give the shop assistant too much money. Do they know what is meant by change?

2 Wall shop

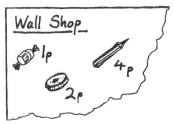

Make a wall display with pictures of low-priced items from catalogues and magazines. This wall shop can be used for oral or written shopping activities. Ask questions such as
'1 biscuit costs 2p. How much do 3 biscuits cost?'
'1 crayon costs 4p. How much do 5 crayons cost?'

3 Bills

Show the children receipts or bills from a supermarket or shop. Ask them what a bill is, why we add it up and how we know how much to pay.

4 Class shop

A class shop is a practical way of giving experience of shopping and adding bills. The children can sell empty grocery packets and tins at low prices as in a sale, or small classroom items such as pencils, crayons, books. The prices can be kept very low at first and in multiples of five pence for larger items. Give the children a certain amount of money to spend. The 'shop assistant' should write out and add up the bill. This may be checked by using a calculator or by the teacher.

5 Change

Talk about what is meant by change, when it is given and why.

6 Shopkeeper's addition

Show the children how to count on to find the change. This is known as shopkeeper's addition. Ask two children to come to the front of the class. One child is the 'customer' and the other the 'shopkeeper'. Give the 'customer' a coin, say 20p, and tell them they have spent 14p. They give the 20p to the 'shopkeeper' who counts out loud from 14p to 20p – handing over the change one coin at a time. The rest of the class can help count out the money.
    This is good practice in mental skills.

MENTAL WORK   Work out change from 10p to reinforce number bonds to 10. Do the same for 20p.

USING A CALCULATOR

Give further practice in entering and adding pence.

24p + 17p

| 2 | 4 | + | 1 | 7 | = |

Children can use calculators for checking bills, with one child adding the coins and another using the calculator and then comparing their answers. They can check their bills for the class shop in this way too.

A game to play

Choose an amount of money such as 25p. This has to be made up exactly to 50p by adding coin values only (20p, 10p, 5p, 2p, 1p) using as few key presses as possible.

LINKS WITH THE ENVIRONMENT

Talk about situations in everyday life which involve paying money. These can be shopping with adults and paying at the supermarket till, or using their own money to buy comics, ice-creams, or to go swimming.

Make a graph to show how much money the children spend each week.

Talk about the times in school when money is collected, such as school trips, savings bank, book club, or dinner money.

Ask the children to look at their parent's bills next time they go shopping. What is the difference between a bill and a receipt?

Have a class fund-raising sale for a favourite charity. This is a good opportunity for practical experience in the use of money.

NOTES ON INVESTIGATIONS

Section A

Do the children find all four possibilities? Are they systematic? For example, do they start with the largest coin first and find all the possibilities for that before moving on to start with the 20p coin?

An extension is to find amounts that could have been lost if a different number of coins had fallen out of the purse.

Section B

Do the children use a system? Do they use the 50p and try all possibilities of making 80p with that? For example,

50p + 20p + 10p   or   50p + 10p + 10p + 10p
or   50p + 10p + 10p + 5p + 5p, . . .

Section C

Remember to review the price of stamps for section C to keep up to date.

Do the children check on the price of first- and second-class stamps before they start? In designing their 50p page of stamps, do they include first- and second-class stamps before including other values? Do they use different stamp values for their other designs?

Number 10

Purpose

To introduce and develop equivalences of halves and quarters

Materials

Strips of paper, squared paper, circles, crayons, scissors, glue, clock stamp, equilateral triangles, rectangles, squares, templates (equilateral triangle, square, pentagon, hexagon, octagon)

Vocabulary

Whole, half, halves, quarter, equal, fraction, square, divide, equilateral triangle, pentagon, hexagon, octagon, templates

TEACHING POINTS

1 Half

Talk about where the children might have heard half before, such as half-time, or half an hour. Remind them that half means two equal parts and show them an example of what is **not** a half. You can do this by tearing a piece of paper into two unequal pieces.

2 Equivalence of halves

Give each child a rectangle of paper. Ask them to write '1 whole' on one side. Tell them to turn it over, fold it in half and write '$\frac{1}{2}$' on each half

Talk about the equivalence of two halves and one whole. Record it as $\frac{2}{2} = 1$

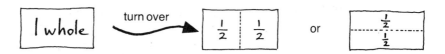

3 Quarters

Talk about how to get quarters by dividing a shape or object into four equal parts. Show the children shapes which are **not** quarters by tearing or cutting a piece of paper into four unequal parts.

4 Equivalence of quarters

Give each child a rectangle of paper. Ask them to write '1 whole' on one side. Tell them to turn it over, fold it into quarters, and write '$\frac{1}{4}$' on each quarter. Talk about the equivalence of four quarters and one whole. Record it as $\frac{4}{4} = 1$

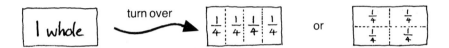

5 Equivalence of halves and quarters

Give the children three equal strips of paper each. Ask them to write '1 whole' on one strip. Tell them to fold and cut the second strip into halves and write '$\frac{1}{2}$' on each piece.

Then tell them to fold and cut the third strip into quarters, and write '$\frac{1}{4}$' on each piece. The children can arrange the pieces to make a fraction wall like this.

I whole			
$\frac{1}{2}$		$\frac{1}{2}$	
$\frac{1}{4}$	$\frac{1}{4}$	$\frac{1}{4}$	$\frac{1}{4}$

Ask the children questions about their walls, such as:
'How many halves match the whole?'
'How many quarters match one half?'
Show a possible way of recording their answers.

$$\frac{2}{2} = 1 \qquad \frac{2}{4} = \frac{1}{2}$$

LINKS WITH THE ENVIRONMENT   Talk with the children about various practical situations involving the equivalence of $\frac{1}{2}$ and $\frac{2}{4}$. These might include cutting an orange into one half and two quarters, or dividing a block of chocolate into halves or quarters. Ask the children to look for circular road signs and window frames which show halves and quarters.

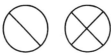 

The clock face can also be used to show the equivalence of $\frac{1}{2} = \frac{2}{4}$.

Section A

Do the children see that each rectangle is $\frac{1}{4}$ of the flag? Do they see that two quarters is half the flag, and that there are several ways of colouring it, such as

In drawing and colouring their own flags, do the children come to understand the equivalence of $\frac{1}{2} = \frac{2}{4}$? Do any of the children draw diagonals to make their flags? If this happens the equivalence may be shown by cutting and superimposing.

Section B

Do the children divide the shape into quarters using one horizontal and one vertical line?

In finding another way to divide the shape into quarters, do the children count the 5 squares in one quarter and find other quarters by counting squares?

Do any of them draw two diagonal lines to divide up the shape into quarters? This solution gives half squares which may need to be discussed. Do the children see that the shapes produced by this method are the same?

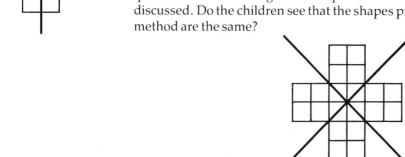

Section C

Do the children divide each shape into half using a ruler?

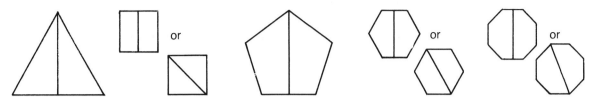

Do the children find that some shapes divide into quarters easily?

Do any children have difficulty dividing the equilateral triangle?

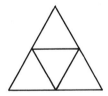

Do the children find that the pentagon cannot easily be divided into quarters?

Length 2

Purpose

- To practise using a ruler
- To introduce measuring and drawing in cm
- To practise estimating

Materials

Rulers, squared paper, string, straws

Vocabulary

Ruler, centimetre (cm), measure, estimate, length, long, longest, shorter, twice

TEACHING POINTS

1 Using the ruler

Talk with the children about the problems when using arbitrary units as they vary from person to person and so why a standard unit that remains constant is needed.

Tell stories about how people used to measure in cubits, for example, Goliath.

Let the children look at a ruler (the dead length type is probably preferable to begin with) and notice how it is marked off in centimetres.

'Why do you think it is better to use centimetres than digits?'

Explain that when we write centimetres, we use cm not cms, e.g. 24 cm.

2 Drawing straight lines

Let the children practise drawing straight lines in cm and writing the measurements on them.

Let the children draw lines for their friends to measure.

Let the children attempt to estimate the lengths of objects in the classroom such as the length of a book. These can then be checked with a ruler. Lots of practice will be needed to get reasonable estimates.

3 The tape measure

Show the children how a tape measure can be used to measure the distance around something like a jam-jar. Talk about why some things need to be measured with a ruler and others with a tape measure.

4 Measuring curved lines

Show the children how to measure a curved line. For example, you can measure it with a piece of string or thread and then measure the string against a ruler. Let the children practise doing this.

Ask the children to measure and cut a piece of string, against their ruler, to a given length such as 12 cm. Then ask them to arrange the string on paper, to draw along it to show a curved line and then to write on the measurement.

5 Classroom measuring

Let the children practise measuring objects in the classroom. Ask them to decide whether to use a ruler or a tape measure.

LINKS WITH THE ENVIRONMENT

Talk about the things we need to measure in everyday life. Talk about buying ribbon, jewellery chains, material, cables and wires.

Talk about measurement in sport, as in high jump and long jump.

Let the children measure the growth of plants such as cress.

Measurement in nature work is always interesting. Find the lengths of the birds which visit the playground and also the lengths of insects. Use these activities for display work. Human as well as animal footprints can be measured for display work.

Talk about when we need to have our feet and other parts of our bodies measured.

Talk about other countries, such as France, which measure in centimetres. Talk about the units that people in Britain used to measure in before centimetres and why we changed.

NOTES ON INVESTIGATIONS

Section A

Do the children understand what is meant by 'twice as big'? Do they just double the length? Do they also understand that the fish must stay in proportion?

Section B

Do the children use a logical approach? Do they check the ages or do they merely choose friends at random? Do they choose a reasonable number of friends? Do they have a system for checking the spans and ages? Do they come to a conclusion?

An extension to this is to display the results and discuss them as a class.

Section C

Do the children consider the lengths of straws they have and plan the shape accordingly? For example, do they use the longest straw as the base line? Do they see the advantage of using centimetre squared paper for this activity?

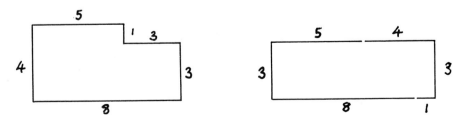

Purpose

- To introduce the gram
- To give practise in weighing and balancing using gram weights

Materials

Balance scales, gram weights, cup, book, plasticine, dried peas, small plastic bags, bowl, wooden spoon, teaspoon, jug, macaroni, labels

Vocabulary

Gram, weigh, weight, heaviest, lightest, less than, balance scales, estimate

TEACHING POINTS

1 Gram weights

Talk about the need for the gram as a standard unit. Let the children handle and compare different gram weights up to, but not including, the 1 kilogram. Some might be confused by the fact that a large number such as 500 g has a relatively light weight. Talk about this.

Children need a lot of practice in estimating weight.

A game to play

GUESS THE WEIGHT

Ask them to estimate weights in grams. Tell them to close their eyes and hold out their hands. Place a weight into their hands and ask if it is heavier than 100 g. Ask them to estimate its weight.

2 Combining weights

Ask the children which weights are needed to make 400 g (200 g, 200 g), and then what other weights could be used (100 g, 100 g, 200 g).

Play the estimating game again but use two or three other weights. Let the children use the balance scales to check their answers.

3 Recording

Introduce the recording of grams as g.

4 Weighing

Ask the children to estimate and then weigh objects using gram weights. Talk about the results: for example,

'Which is the heaviest?'
'Which is the lightest?'

MENTAL WORK Give the children practice in adding the gram weights they will be using for their weighing activities such as 100 g + 100 g = 200 g.

LINKS WITH THE ENVIRONMENT Talk with the children about where they might see things weighed or marked in grams.

- At the grocer's shop or supermarket the weight of tins, boxes and packets are all marked in grams.
- At the sweet shop they might buy sweets and have them weighed in grams.
- At home some of the ingredients for a recipe might be weighed in grams.

Collect tins, packets and boxes which are marked in grams and make a display. Pictures may also be used.

NOTES ON INVESTIGATIONS **Section A**

Do the children try the largest weight first and then add others to balance 200 g? Do they try all possible combinations? For example,

100 g + 100 g = 200 g
100 g + 50 g + 50 g = 200 g
50 g + 50 g + 50 g + 50 g = 200 g

Do they then try to find other sets of weights? For example,

100 g + 50 g + 20 g + 20 g + 10 g = 200 g

Section B

In making the 150 g of plasticine, do the children balance their 50 g bag with 50 g of plasticine three times and put the plasticine together like this: 50 g + 50 g + 50 g = 150 g? Do they put their 200 g and 50 g bags on different sides of the balance scales and add plasticine onto the 50 g side until they balance?

To make 100 g of plasticine do they balance 50 g of plasticine twice against their own 50 g bag? Do any of the children make use of the 150 g of plasticine they have just made? For example,
200 g + 50 g = 150 g + 100 g.

Section C

Do the children choose a weight for their lunch packs before finding food to match? Or do they do it by balancing the weights of food? For example,

200 g (banana) + 150 g (apple)   weigh the same as 350 g (drink)

Do they use multiples of certain foods? For example, two packets of crisps (50 g).

Volume and capacity 2

Purpose

To introduce the litre and $\frac{1}{2}$ litre

Materials

Water, litre measure, $\frac{1}{2}$ litre measure, cup, beaker, mug, litre bottle, jug, yogurt pot, teapot, kettle, bucket, selection of containers (some 1 litre, some more, some less)

Vocabulary

Litre measure, litre container, half litre, pour, measure, estimate, check, shape, more, less, quarter litre, fill

TEACHING POINTS

1 The standard measure

Ask the children to think about when it is important to measure liquids accurately such as in cooking and buying petrol. Talk about how jugs vary and how we need a standard measuring jug if we are to measure accurately.

2 The litre measure

Show the children a litre jug and ask how many of them have seen one at home. Point out the litre line and explain that if the liquid is level with it, then there is a litre of liquid in the jug. Give practise in filling the jug to the litre mark.

Let the children experiment by pouring a litre of water into different sized and shaped containers so that they see the different forms a litre may take.

Look at different popular soft drink containers to see how many hold a litre.

Let the children estimate and measure how many glasses or beakers they can fill from a litre bottle of water.

3 The half litre

Fill a litre measure with water. Pour half of it into a half litre measure. Ask the children to measure what is left.

Pour the half litre back into the litre measure. Ask them what two half litres make.

Let the children find containers they estimate might hold a half litre and then check them by pouring in a half litre of water. Talk with them about how accurate their estimates were.

A game to play

Let one child choose a partner and select a container. The partner guesses how much it holds. The first player checks the capacity. This could be extended to a team game with points being scored.

LINKS WITH THE ENVIRONMENT

Talk about how many measured liquids we use in everyday life.

- Bottles of drinks, cartons of orange.
- Milk comes in either bottles or cartons.
- Petrol. How many litres do parents buy when they stop at a garage?
- Compare the capacity of car petrol tanks, using magazine data or personal knowledge. Oil for cars might also be discussed.
- Paint and glue containers in the classroom.
- Other containers such as bottles of shampoo, hand-cream, washing-up liquid.

Why is it important that these liquids are in measured amounts?

NOTES ON INVESTIGATIONS

Section A

Do the children make realistic choices? Do they make reasonable estimates of more than a litre of water? Do they look for several examples? Do they include some large amounts such as bath water?

Section B

Do the children estimate and select possible containers, eliminating some (such as an egg cup) immediately? Do they check their choices by using a litre measure? If the container is too small do they stop pouring before it overflows? Do they appreciate that a litre of water can take any shape? Are they able to explain this in a sentence?

Section C

Do the children realise that there are about four mugs to the litre? Do they count up how many mugs of liquid they drink at each meal? Do they remember to add on the extra drinks they have after school and at supper time? Do they understand that they have to divide the numbers of mugs by 4 to find the number of litres? How do they find out how many litres their friends drink?

This investigation might be extended to finding how much liquid is drunk in a month, or a year.

Purpose

- To revise or introduce o'clock, half past and quarter past the hour
- To introduce digital o'clock times

Materials

Clock faces, digital watch or clock, clock stamp, crayons

Vocabulary

O'clock, half past, quarter past, times, before, after, order, digital, hour

TEACHING POINTS

1 Telling the time

Talk to the children about the sort of clocks they see, such as kitchen clocks, alarm clocks, church clocks, grandfather clocks.

Ask what type of watches they have, digital or ones with face and hands.

Collect pictures or make a frieze showing different types of clocks.

2 Clock faces

Talk about the position and numbers on the clock face. A demonstration or real clock is useful.

Talk about the minute and hour hand. Show the movement of the hands. An actual clock is useful for this.

Show the children how to use a clock stamp.

3 O'clock

Talk with the children about o'clock times, Show them an hour by moving the minute hand round once.

Set the hands of the clock to various times such as 9 o'clock and ask the children what time this is.

Talk about what numbers the hour hand and minute hand are pointing to.

Ask them what time it will be in another hour.

Relate the times shown on the clock face to everyday happenings. For example, school starts at 9 o'clock, and lunch time is 12 o'clock.

Hold a ruler in one hand to represent the minute hand and turn your back to the class. Hold your hands at o'clock times. Ask the children to tell the times shown. Individual children may show times in the same way.

Show the children how to record o'clock times.

4 Digital o'clock

Talk about digital o'clock and how to write it. For example 10:00.

5 Half past

Revise or introduce half past. Show on a demonstration clock what happens to the hands. The half can be related to fractions of a circle.

Repeat the 'ruler clock' activity above.

Show the children how to record half past times.

Relate the times to everyday happenings. For example, play time is half past ten, and half past three is time to go home from school.

6 Quarter past

Use similar activities to teach quarter past. Show the recording.

Two circles of different coloured card can be made. Both are cut to the centre.

When they are slotted together, o'clock, half past and quarter past can be shown.

MENTAL WORK   Show children times on the clock face. Ask what the time will be one hour before/after this.

LINKS WITH THE ENVIRONMENT

Talk about the different types of clocks we see in the environment.

- On the way to school – clocks in jeweller's shop windows, church clock, town hall clock, bus station clock
- In school – school hall clock, classroom clock, equipment for time
- At home – clock radio, dining room clock, alarm clock, cooker clock.

A display of pictures of clocks can be made from catalogue pictures.

NOTES ON INVESTIGATIONS

Section A

Do the children's choice of four times match up with their pictures? Are the activities shown in the correct order? For example, get up, then have breakfast.

Section B

Do the children colour half an hour by drawing a line from 12 to 6? Do the children colour another half hour by drawing a line from 3 to 9? Do the children see that drawing lines 1 to 7, 2 to 8, 3 to 9, 4 to 10, 5 to 11 and 6 to 12 would all show half an hour? Do the children draw half an hour in any other way? Show them that any straight line drawn through the centre of the circle produces half an hour.

Section C

Do the children see that the pattern on their clocks produces a square? Do they work through the numbers in order? Do they see that the pattern increases in threes?

$$12 \rightarrow 3 \rightarrow 6 \rightarrow 9 \rightarrow 12, \quad 1 \rightarrow 4 \rightarrow 7 \rightarrow 10 \rightarrow 1, \quad 2 \rightarrow 5 \rightarrow 8 \rightarrow 11 \rightarrow 2.$$

Angles 2

Purpose

- To revise left and right
- To introduce $\frac{1}{2}$ and $\frac{1}{4}$ turns

Materials

Clock face, tracing paper, squared paper, circles, paper fastener

Vocabulary

Full turn, right, left, quarter, half, direction, forward, instructions

TEACHING POINTS

1 Half turns

Ask the children to face the front of the room and then make a half turn. What do they face now? Which way did they turn? To the right or to the left?

2 Half and quarter turns

Talk about half and quarter turns to the right and left.

A game to play

Give a child instructions to follow.
'Make a quarter turn to the left then a half turn to the right. What are you facing now?'

3 On the clock

Use a clock face and a folded paper circle to show quarters and right-angles.

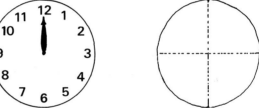

Ask what number the hand points to if it makes a quarter turn to the right. Then ask what it points to if it makes a quarter turn to the left.

4 Planning routes

Talk with the children about how to show a route around the school or across the classroom.
They can plot routes on squared paper. Different starting points might be used. Instructions should be written:

(1) Go forward 2 and make $\frac{1}{4}$ turn right
(2) Go forward 3 and make $\frac{1}{4}$ turn left
(3) Go forward 1 . . .

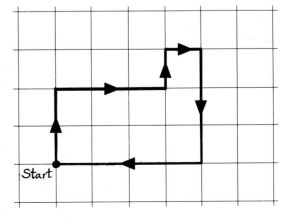

A game to play

Give a child instructions:
'Take 3 paces forward and make a quarter turn right.'
'Now take 4 paces forward and make a quarter turn left.'
'Where are you now?'

5 Turtle

A turtle (computer-controlled robot) might also be used to show these ideas.

MENTAL WORK   Ask the children questions about left or right positions in the classroom, such as 'Who is sitting on Sarah's left?'.

LINKS WITH THE ENVIRONMENT   Ask the children to think of times when we meet quarter turns to the left and to the right. Talk about waiting at traffic lights to turn left or right at crossroads.

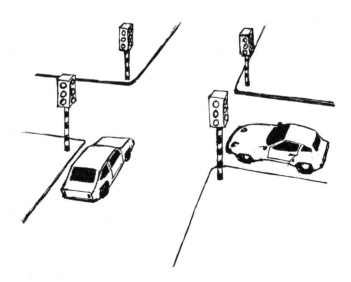

Can they plan how to turn a car round on a road which does not allow U turns? Draw a plan like the one below. Discuss how we turn $\frac{1}{4}$ right, $\frac{1}{4}$ right, $\frac{1}{4}$ right, $\frac{1}{4}$ left to get back on the road travelling in the opposite direction.

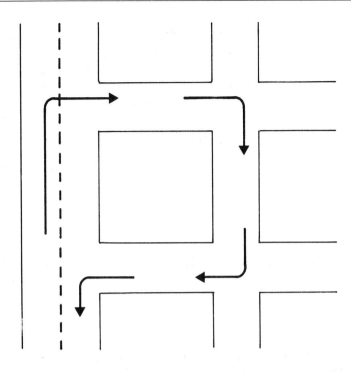

NOTES ON INVESTIGATIONS

Section A

Do the children know the difference between left and right? Do they make up moves for their friends and give the correct answers?

Section B

Do the children use the correct notation to move the turtle? Do they show starting and stopping points? Do their directions make the shapes drawn?

Section C

Do the children draw a closed shape such as this on squared paper? Do they choose different starting points? Do they go both clockwise and anti-clockwise?

Number 11

Purpose

- To develop an awareness of number patterns
- To practise addition of HTU with exchange or 'carrying' to the tens
- To introduce magic squares to give practice in addition

Materials

100 square or 100 board, structural apparatus, magic squares, squared paper, calculator

Vocabulary

Pattern, magic square, magic number, calculator, number pattern, score, across, down, cross-number puzzle, line, crosses, solve, clues

TEACHING POINTS

1 Patterns

Talk about patterns. Ask what a pattern is, and then for examples of patterns on children's clothes and in the classroom.

Ask how numbers can make a pattern. Encourage children to suggest different number patterns and to say why they are patterns.

Make a number pattern round the class by asking every third child to stand up.

Ask the children if they can make a pattern on the calculator. Press, for example, $\boxed{+}$ $\boxed{2}$ each time or use the constant function.

2 100 square

Look for patterns on the 100 square or 100 board. Use a class 100 square or give the children individual copies.
Ask them to find numbers like 7, 17, 27, 37, . . .
'Where do we find numbers ending in 5?'
Can they make patterns by adding 5 or 10?

1	2	3	4	5	6	7	8	9	10
11	12	13	14	15	16	17	18	19	20
21	22	23	24	25	26	27	28	29	30
31	32	33	34	35	36	37	38	39	40

Children usually enjoy looking for different patterns on the square. Let them colour some of the patterns or transfer the numbers to pattern snakes.

A game to play

Make a number pattern and give one number to each child: for example,

7, 17, 27, . . . , 97
5, 15, 25, . . . , 95

Go into the hall or yard. At a given signal, children find the others in their pattern and line up in the correct order.

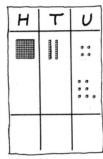

$$\begin{array}{r} H\ T\ U \\ 1\ 2\ 4 \\ +\qquad 7 \\ \hline \\ \hline \end{array}$$

3 Addition of HTU with 'carrying' or exchanging

Use structural apparatus to show this.
    Give further examples and sometimes ask the children to set up the apparatus.

4 Pattern in addition of HTU

Ask the children if they can see a pattern in addition:
For example, add another ten, the tens number is one greater, and if they add another hundred, the hundreds number is one greater.

$$\begin{array}{r} 375 \\ +\quad 8 \\ \hline 383 \end{array} \qquad \begin{array}{r} 375 \\ +\ 18 \\ \hline 393 \end{array} \qquad \begin{array}{r} 375 \\ +\ 118 \\ \hline 493 \end{array}$$

A game to play

Prepare cards, some marked with 100 and some with 10. Put them in a bag or box. Write a number on the board such as 126. Ask a child to choose a number from the bag and then add it to the number on the board. Let other children do this, adding to the same number each time.

5 Magic squares and crosses

The magic square originated in China. Magic squares or crosses are a useful method of encouraging children to practise addition in a fun way. Adding each line gives the same 'magic number'. Let the children discover this for themselves.

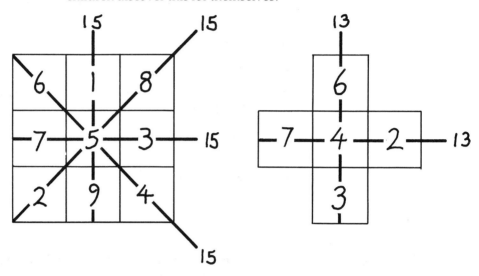

Talk about how to complete magic squares. First find the magic number.

$8 + 7 + 6 = 21$
$8 + \square + 10 = 21$ so $\square = 3$
$3 + 7 + \square = 21$ so $\square = 11$

8		10
9	7	
4		6

MENTAL WORK   Discuss with the children the strategy for adding 10, 20, 30, . . . to a number. Extend this to adding 100, 200, . . .

Ask children to complete patterns such as 2, 4, 6, 8, . . . and to state what the pattern is.

Discuss the addition pattern of adding 9, 19, . . .

USING THE   Let the children practise adding three-digit numbers.
CALCULATOR   Show them how to use the constant function. Calculators can vary with the make and the teacher should be familiar with the different possibilities if children are allowed to use their own calculators.

For example: pressing the $=$ button repeatedly often makes the calculator carry on doing the operations, for example 3 $+$ 3 $=$ $=$ $=$ $=$ $=$ . . .

If not 3 $+$ $+$ 3 $=$ $=$ $=$ $=$ $=$ $=$ . . . may be required.

A game to play

AIM FOR 999

Ask the children to enter a given number. They have three moves to reach 999 by adding three numbers. For example:

123 + 800 + 70 + 6 = 999
456 + 3 + 40 + 500 = 999

A simpler game is to aim for 99.

LINKS WITH THE ENVIRONMENT

Ask children to look for number patterns that they see in everyday use such as sequences of numbers on houses and on pages of books.

Look at number patterns on game boards. How does a snakes and ladders board differ from the 100 square that the children have been using? Look for a number pattern, for example, on dice (opposite faces add up to 7).

Discuss where they might find other number patterns in games and sport, such as numbers on football team jerseys.

NOTES ON INVESTIGATIONS

Section A

Do children see the pattern in questions 9 to 16? Do they make a similar pattern by increasing the lower number each time?

Section B

Do the children see that the smallest number they can make by adding is 3 + 3 = 6, then 3 + 5 = 8, then 3 + 3 + 3 = 9? Do they use a trial-and-error approach? Or do they work through the numbers in order?

10 = 5 + 5	16 = 5 + 5 + 3 + 3
11 = 5 + 3 + 3	17 = 5 + 3 + 3 + 3 + 3
12 = 3 + 3 + 3 + 3	18 = 5 + 5 + 5 + 3
13 = 5 + 5 + 3	19 = 5 + 5 + 3 + 3 + 3
14 = 5 + 3 + 3 + 3	20 = 5 + 5 + 5 + 5
15 = 5 + 5 + 5	

NB. Children may find alternative answers for some numbers.

Do they list the numbers they cannot make by adding 3s and 5s?

An extension activity is to use two numbers other than 3 and 5.

Section C

There are many correct answers. Do the children understand that the numbers in the cross-number square are the *answers* and that they must think of the clues? For example

1. Across ☐ + ☐ = 136

Talk to the children about answers that are possible here and what would be an 'efficient' way of going about this, such as putting a number like 100 in the first box. Think about using a calculator for this.

Purpose

- To develop number pattern awareness
- To introduce subtraction of hundreds, tens and units with decomposition from the tens

Materials

100 squares, crayons, structural apparatus, squared paper, calculator

Vocabulary

Count back, subtract, difference between, minus, 100 square, puzzle, subtraction

TEACHING POINTS   **1 Patterns**

Ask the children to look at the 100 square and point out patterns which they can see.

1	2	3	4	5	6	7	8	9	10
11	12	13	14	15	16	17	18	19	20
21	22	23	24	25	26	27	28	29	30
31	32	33	34	35	36	37	38	39	40
41	42	43	44	45	46	47	48	49	50
51	52	53	54	55	56	57	58	59	60
61	62	63	64	65	66	67	68	69	70
71	72	73	74	75	76	77	78	79	80
81	82	83	84	85	86	87	88	89	90
91	92	93	94	95	96	97	98	99	100

Talk about subtraction patterns on the 100 square.
Show the children how each hop this way subtracts 1,

and each hop this way subtracts 10.

Ask them to count down in 10s from 95 to 5. What do they notice?
Ask them to colour subtractions patterns on the 100 square and
record the numbers.
Talk about other subtraction patterns. For example, what patterns
can they see here?

$$17 - 8 = 9 \qquad 47 - 8 = 39$$
$$27 - 8 = 19 \qquad 57 - 8 = 49$$
$$37 - 8 = 29$$

What patterns do they get if they subtract in tens?

100, 90, 80, 70, . . .
95, 85, 75, 65, . . .
91, 81, 71, 61, . . .

The calculator may be used for some of this work.

2 Vertical recording

Show the children the vertical recording of subtraction. Use structural
apparatus to give the necessary imagery. Teachers will wish to make
their own decision about the words they use for this.

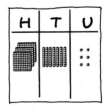

The position of the subtraction sign should be pointed out to the
children:

H T U   H T U
3 7 6   3 7 6
−   5 and not − 5
─────   ─────

3 Horizontal to vertical recording

Show how to move from the horizontal to the vertical form of
recording. Remind the children to place the numbers in the right
column.

$$H\ T\ U$$
$$458 - 26 \longrightarrow \begin{array}{r} 458 \\ -\ 26 \\ \hline \end{array}$$

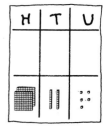

4 Decomposition from the tens

Use structural apparatus to remind the children about decomposition.

Remind them how to record it.

$$\begin{array}{ccc} H\ T\ U & H\ T\ U & H\ T\ U \\ 2\ \ 5\ \ 3 & 2\ {}^4\!5\ {}^1\!3 & 2\ {}^4\!5\ {}^1\!3 \\ -\ \ \ 2\ 8 & -\ \ \ 2\ 8 & -\ \ \ 2\ 8 \\ \hline & & 2\ 2\ 5 \end{array}$$

Teachers will obviously wish to use their own words and methods for this. The important point is to use some imagery to explain what is happening.

5 Linking addition and subtraction

Talk about the link between addition and subtraction.

$$\begin{array}{lll} 3 + 4 = 7 & 11 + 12 = 23 & 315 + 121 = 436 \\ 4 + 3 = 7 & 12 + 11 = 23 & 121 + 315 = 436 \\ 7 - 3 = 4 & 23 - 11 = 12 & 436 - 121 = 315 \\ 7 - 4 = 3 & 23 - 12 = 11 & 436 - 315 = 121 \end{array}$$

A game to play

NUMBER HUNT

Give the children a number, such as 20. Ask them to write as many different addition and subtraction bonds using that number in two minutes as they can. For example, suppose the number chosen is 20.

$$\begin{array}{llll} 19 + 1 = 20 & 6 + 14 = 20 & 9 + 11 = 20 & 13 + 7 = 20 \\ 1 + 19 = 20 & 20 - 6 = 14 & 11 + 9 = 20 & \text{etc.} \end{array}$$

$$20 - 1 = 19 \quad 20 - 14 = 6 \quad 20 - 11 = 9$$
$$20 - 19 = 1 \quad 14 + 6 = 20 \quad 20 - 9 = 11$$

The winner is the one with the most correct number bonds.

Try to encourage the children to use the link between addition and subtraction to find number bonds.

MENTAL WORK Ask the children subtraction questions using the words 'take away', 'minus', 'subtract'.

Ask them to continue subtraction patterns such as $54 - 6 = 48$, $44 - 6 = 38$ and so on.

Discuss the strategy for subtracting 9, 19, . . .

USING THE CALCULATOR Encourage the children to use the calculator to discover subtraction patterns. For example:

100, 90, 80, 70, . . .
100, 95, 90, 85, . . .

Larger numbers may also be introduced.

500, 400, 300, . . .
450, 400, 350, . . .

Let the children practise subtraction using the calculator.

$296 - 74$
$347 - 125$

A game to play

TARGET ZERO

Two players use one calculator. The first player enters a three-digit number into the calculator. The second player 'shoots down' one digit at a time until zero is reached in three subtractions.

$$829 - 9 \quad = 820$$
$$820 - 20 = 800$$
$$800 - 800 = 0$$

LINKS WITH THE ENVIRONMENT Talk with the children about where we might meet subtraction situations involving larger numbers in everyday life. These might include subtraction from 301 or 501 in a game of darts, the number of shopping days (or just days) left to Christmas, or the number of minutes left to play in a football match.

NOTES ON INVESTIGATIONS

Section A

Do the children have difficulty in finding the numbers on the 100 square? (Some children might find it helpful to mark the 2×2 or 3×3 square on the 100 square first.) Do any of the children find the missing numbers without using the 100 square, by understanding the pattern?

The investigation can be extended by asking children to use a 4×4 or 5×5 square in the same way.

Section B

The children could use a calculator for this investigation. Do they use a method to find subtractions?

$$125 - 1, \quad 126 - 2, \quad 127 - 3, \quad 128 - 4, \quad 129 - 5, \text{ etc.}$$

Section C

Do the children find ways of making different 100 squares? For example, writing the numbers forwards and backwards, or in a spiral.

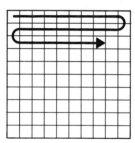 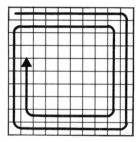

Do they see any number patterns in their 100 squares?

This can be extended by starting in different ways, for example, starting by numbering a diagonal.

Shape 3

Purpose

- To introduce bilateral symmetry
- To relate symmetry to the environment

Materials

Scissors, glue, paper, crayons, squared paper

Vocabulary

Symmetry, line of symmetry, symmetrical, half, squares, shape, fold, pattern, squared paper

TEACHING POINTS   **1 Making symmetrical shapes**

Talk to the children about how a shape is symmetrical if it can be folded in half to fit exactly on itself. Let the children experience this with folding and cutting activities. Ask them to fold paper into half and cut out various shapes from the fold. Ask them why the shapes *and* the remaining frames are symmetrical. The cut out shapes can be used for display.

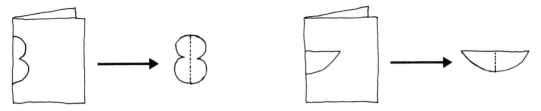

Black shapes can be mounted on white paper.

Talk with the children about what happens if we do not fold the paper exactly in half but still cut out from the fold. Do they see that the symmetry of the shape depends on cutting out from the fold?

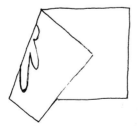 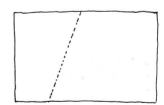

2 Line of symmetry

Tell the children that the fold line is called the line of symmetry. Ask them to draw the line of symmetry on their cut-out shape.

3 Blob pattern symmetry

Drop blobs of paint onto paper, fold once and open the paper up again to see the symmetrical shape.

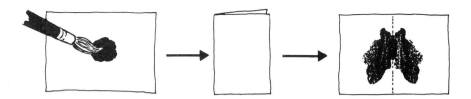

4 Shapes without symmetry

Look at simple shapes in the classroom which have not got symmetry. What needs to be added to give them symmetry?

Ask the children to look in a mirror to see if their face has symmetry. Is it exactly the same on both sides? What about their hair parting?

Let the children draw a clown's face without symmetry. Then let them ask a friend to add something to give it symmetry.

LINKS WITH THE ENVIRONMENT

Consider how symmetry occurs naturally and how we deliberately build it into our environment.

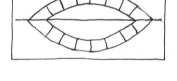

- Birds and butterflies, for example, are symmetrical or they would not be able to fly efficiently. This principle is used in the design of aeroplanes.
- Our bodies, too are more or less symmetrical so that we are balanced when we walk. Ask the children, for example, what would be the effect if one of our legs was very much longer than the other.
- Talk about balance in the PE lesson.
- Look for symmetrical shapes in the classroom.
- Look for photographs of reflections on water.

Use symmetry ideas in art work:

- Cut out symmetrical butterflies from folded paper. Put blobs of paint on them and fold them up again to give a symmetrical pattern on the wings.
- Cut out symmetrical shapes such as Christmas trees or snowmen for friezes or mobiles.

NOTES ON INVESTIGATIONS

Section A

Use squared paper for this investigation. Are the children aware of the 'balance' involved in bilateral symmetry? Talk about how many squares in the shape and how they are arranged to balance each other. Do the children see that there must be six squares on either side of the line of symmetry? Do any children, when making their own shape, draw in a line of symmetry to begin with and then work out from this line by placing squares to balance those on the other side of the line?

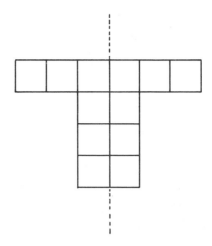

Section B

Do the children show that they understand the principle of symmetry? Do they look at the two squares on the top line and make the pattern symmetrical? Do they start one square away so that they will be balanced. Does their colouring have symmetry?

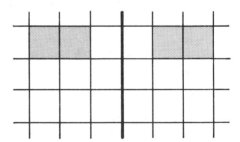

Section C

Do the children put two of the shapes together to make one shape with symmetry? Do they use them again to make different symmetrical shapes? Do they draw them on squared paper and correctly show each line of symmetry? Possible solutions include:

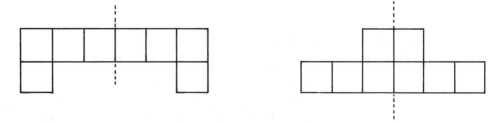

An extension activity is to make a symmetrical shape using four of the shapes.

Number 13

Purpose

- To introduce vertical recording of multiplication
- To give practice in multiplication
- To link addition and multiplication

Materials

Structural apparatus, squared paper

Vocabulary

Different, double, outside, middle, sets of

TEACHING POINTS

1 Linking addition and multiplication

Ask children to think of another way of writing 5 + 5, for example,

2 sets of 5
2×5

Explain to children that 2 sets of 5 has the same answer as 5 sets of 2.

2 Recording

Link addition, multiplication and the commutative property by showing the different ways of recording them.

$$
\begin{array}{ccccc}
\text{TU} & & \text{TU} & & \text{TU} \\
5 & & 2 & & 5 \\
+\ \underline{5} & \text{or} \ \times & \underline{5} & \text{or} \ \times & \underline{2} \\
\underline{} & & \underline{} & & \underline{}
\end{array}
$$

Let the children practise this by making a game of it where they write out other examples such as 3 + 3 and give them to a friend to write out the three ways.

3 Structural apparatus

Use structural apparatus to give children the necessary imagery. Remind them that they must place the numbers in the correct columns. Squared paper is useful for this at first.

The children might like to check their answers on a calculator.

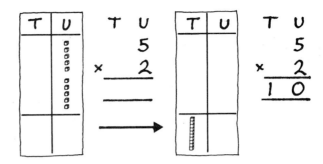

MENTAL WORK   Ask the children multiplication bonds, including simple verbal problems, such as '3 children each have 2 sweets. How many sweets have they altogether?'

USING THE CALCULATOR   Children should continue to practise simple multiplication of one digit by one digit. They might set multiplication problems for their friends and check the answers on their calculators.

×	1	2	3	4	5
1	1				
2		4			
3			9		
4				16	
5					25

A game to play

Use a multiplication square. Multiply the numbers 1, 2, 3, 4, 5, . . . by themselves and colour in the answers. What pattern do the children get?

LINKS WITH THE ENVIRONMENT   Encourage children to look about them for objects that come in groups such as eggs in boxes, buttons on cards, crayons in packets, notelets in boxes.

Look for games where the score is doubled or trebled such as Scrabble and darts.

NOTES ON
INVESTIGATIONS

Section A

Talk to the children about how this might be tackled. Do the children realise that they have to make rectangles? Do they find several ways of doing this? Talk about using a multiplication square to find the answers.

Section B

Do the children look for a pattern in the three numbers? For example, the outside numbers are $+3$ and -3 from the middle number. Do the children discover this will work for any number? For example, if they try 12 they get $12 - 3 = 9$ and $12 + 3 = 15$. So 9, 12 and 15 work. Will it work if they add and subtract a number greater than 3? Let the children build up a number of trios of numbers of this sort.

Extend the problem: for example, 'The outside numbers are 4 and 14. How do we find the middle number?'

Section C

Do the children work by trial and error or do they use a system? One method might be to first use only the twos:

> 2×2
> $2 \times 2 \times 2$
> $2 \times 2 \times 2 \times 2$

Then try the threes, and the fives, and finally combinations of numbers.

Purpose

To measure area by counting whole squares and half squares

Materials

Crayons, squared paper

Vocabulary

Area, squares, half, triangle, rectangle, larger

TEACHING POINTS

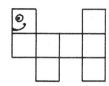

1 Counting whole squares

Talk with the children about finding the area of shapes by counting whole squares. Draw some pictures or shapes made from whole squares. Record the area.

2 Half squares

Show the children how to measure area by counting whole and half squares.

Look at the different ways of dividing a square in half diagonally.

Draw a picture which includes some half squares. Ask the children how many whole and how many half squares there are.

3 Recording

Record the area as

Area = ☐ squares

It might help some children with counting if the whole squares are marked with a dot or coloured in some way.

4 Pictures and patterns

Ask the children to draw a picture or pattern which includes half squares and record the area. Ask them to draw their own pictures or patterns with a given area such as $21\frac{1}{2}$ squares. The fact that these pictures or patterns with a 'fixed' area have different shapes may lead to an interesting discussion. This is, of course, the principle of the conservation of area.

LINKS WITH THE ENVIRONMENT

Talk with the children about where we might see shapes with whole and half squares in the environment.

On the way to school we might see garden paths and patios made from whole and half squares. Some flagstones are made from whole and half squares.

Talk about where whole and half squares might be seen at home. For example, wallpaper designs, tiling in the kitchen or bathroom.

In school, art work might include making pictures from gummed paper squares and half squares. Display some of the above shapes, or pictures of them, and record their areas.

NOTES ON INVESTIGATIONS

Section A

Do the children realise that they can draw many shapes with the same area? Do the children count each area correctly? Do they use half squares? Do they mark the whole squares as they count them?

Section B

Do the children count the areas of the three triangles correctly?

A = 4 squares, B = 4 squares, C = 8 squares

Do the children need reminding about the shape of a rectangle? Do they realise that the area of the rectangle is the same as the area of the original square because it uses all the three pieces? Do the children realise that the three triangles are related? i.e.

area of triangle A = area of triangle B = half the area of triangle C.

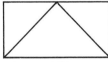
Area = 16 squares

Area = 8 squares

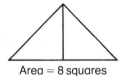
Area = 8 squares

Section C

Area = ½ square

Do the children use the lines on the squared paper to help in drawing the triangles? Do they divide the squares into half diagonally? Do they try drawing half squares together in order to draw some of their triangles?

Area = 1 square

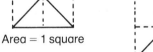
Area = 2 squares

Do they find other triangles?

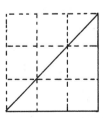

or

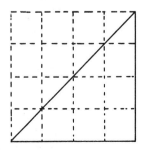

Number 14

Purpose

To introduce vertical recording of multiplication of two digits by one digit (answers in tens and units only)

Materials

Structural apparatus, calculator

Vocabulary

Multiply, pairs, different, groups of, sets of

TEACHING POINTS

1 Structural apparatus

Talk with the children about how 3×5 means 3 sets of 5. Can they think of another way of finding the answer? For example, 5 sets of 3.

Do they understand that 2×23 means 2 sets of 23? Show them how to record this.

```
  T U
  2 3
×   2
  ───
```

Use structural apparatus to give appropriate imagery.

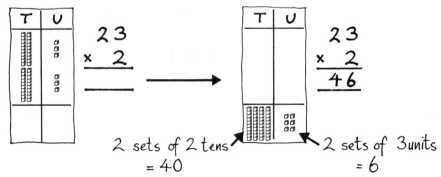

Make the point to children that we are finding 2 sets of 3 units and then 2 sets of 2 tens. This is known as the distributive property of multiplication:

$$2 \times 23 = (2 \times 20) + (2 \times 3)$$

Use structural apparatus to explain this as it is an important property of number.

2 Exchanging or carrying

Talk about what happens in the case of

$$
\begin{array}{r}
\text{T U} \\
2\ 7 \\
\times \quad 2 \\
\hline
\end{array}
$$

This can be shown using structural apparatus.

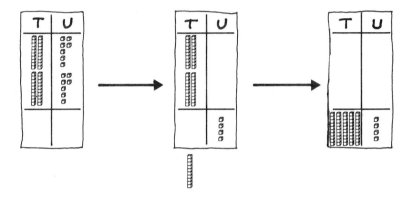

This is one method of setting it down:

$$
\begin{array}{r}
\text{T U} \\
2\ 7 \\
\times \quad 2 \\
\hline
\end{array}
\rightarrow
\begin{array}{r}
\text{T U} \\
2\ 7 \\
\times \quad 2 \\
\hline
4 \\
1
\end{array}
\rightarrow
\begin{array}{r}
\text{T U} \\
2\ 7 \\
\times \quad 2 \\
\hline
5\ 4 \\
1
\end{array}
$$

You may have your own preference as to where the exchange or 'carrying' figure is placed:

$$
\begin{array}{r}
\text{T U} \\
2\ 7 \\
\times \quad 2 \\
\hline
1
\end{array}
\quad \text{or} \quad
\begin{array}{r}
\text{T U} \\
2\ 7 \\
\times\ {}_1\ 2 \\
\hline
\end{array}
$$

MENTAL WORK   Continue to practise simple multiplication bonds. Extend to 20×2, 20×3. Discuss how 2×24 is $2 \times 20 + 2 \times 4$.

USING THE CALCULATOR   Give multiplication practise on the calculator. Ask the children to work out 5×14. Can they press the keys in a different order and still get the same answer? Do they realise that 5 sets of 14 is the same as 14 sets of 5? Let the children try other one digit × two digit problems to reinforce the commutative property. For example

23 × 2 = 46   2 × 23 = 46

A game to play

Two children are each given a calculator and the numbers 2, 3 and 4. The winner is the first to make the highest number they can using 2, 3, 4 and ×; for example,

23 × 4   43 × 2

LINKS WITH THE ENVIRONMENT

Look for objects in the environment that come in sets, such as four wheels on cars, two wheels on bicycles, shoes in pairs in shoe shops.

How many shoes are worn by all children in the class?

Count cars in the school car-park, and ask how many wheels, doors, etc. on all the cars?

NOTES ON INVESTIGATIONS

Section A

Do the children pick any two numbers and multiply them, then see if the others will fit in? Ask them if they think that this is a good way to do it. Talk about the disadvantages of trial-and-error methods. Can they suggest other ways?

One method might be to write the numbers in ascending order and look for pairs that give the same answer when multiplied.

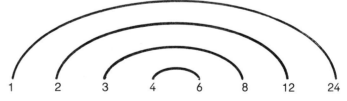

1   2   3   4   6   8   12   24

Section B

Do the children start at 1, then 2, etc. and check on the calculator to see if these are factors? Do they write the numbers as they try each one?

1 × 48 = 48
2 × 24 = 48
3 × 16 = 48
4 × 12 = 48
5
6 × 8 = 48
7
etc.

Section C

Do the children start with the three smallest numbers first?

$$1 \times 2 \times 3 = 6$$

Do they try all possibilities for 1 and 2 before trying other numbers?

$$1 \times 2 \times 3 = 6$$
$$1 \times 2 \times 4 = 8$$
$$1 \times 2 \times 5$$
$$1 \times 2 \times 6$$
etc.

Data 3

Purpose

- To revise block graphs
- To introduce the 1:2 scale
- To encourage children to use graphs to interpret data

Materials

Squared paper

Vocabulary

Block graph, fewest, most, same, altogether, more, fewer, longest, title, labels, savings, number

TEACHING POINTS

1 Block graphs using the 1:1 scale

Revise the drawing of block graphs and the numbering and labelling of axes. This can be done by drawing a block graph of, for example, pets and asking the children to put in the information. Talk about how a graph gives information in an easy-to-read form.

2 The 1:2 scale

Point out that on the last graph drawn the scale is 1:1 and ask what we can do if the numbers up the side are too big to fit on the paper (for example, numbers of children in school classes). Complete a table and use this to introduce the 1:2 scale in order to get all the information on the graph.

3 Asking questions

Ask the children some questions about the graph. Can they think of any more questions themselves? Try to include at least one open-ended question that will encourage the children to reflect. For example, 'Why do you think that . . . ?' It might also be worth talking about the type of graph in section C, where there is a build-up of data.

USING THE CALCULATOR

Talk about the pattern of twos, linking this with the 1:2 scale, and use the constant function on the calculator:

> 1 press   → 2
> 2 presses → 4
> 3 presses → 6

LINKS WITH THE ENVIRONMENT

Link graphs with other areas of the curriculum. Talk about:

- Sport: sports scores to compare weekly games
- Traffic surveys: numbers of cars, buses, lorries
- Nature survey: creatures found – snails, ladybirds
- Shop or house survey: types found or seen
- Spending: amounts of money spent on different activities
- Social: favourite books, sports, lessons

NOTES ON INVESTIGATIONS

Section A

Do the children write a suitable title for the graph to fit the numbers? Do they label the graph correctly? Do the questions match the information given on the graph? Are they open or closed questions? Is the table filled in correctly?

Section B

Do the children appreciate the problem of the large number of stamps? Do they choose the more appropriate graph? Are they able to give a sensible reason for doing this? (For example, that it is too 'tall' for a 1:1 scale.) Do they draw the graph and label it correctly?

Section C

Do the children complete both graphs correctly? Do they understand the different scales involved, i.e. 1:1 and 1:2? Do they understand that the same information can be used with different scales?

Purpose

- To introduce the pound and the notation for pounds and pence
- To introduce addition and subtraction of pounds and pence: exchange or 'carrying' in the units column for addition and no decomposition in subtraction

Materials

Coins

Vocabulary

Coins, pound, pennies, pence, saves, savings, least, most, spend, money, total, bank, bank books, buy

TEACHING POINTS

1 £1 coin

Ask the children what one hundred pennies make. Talk about how awkward it would be to carry all our money in small change and why we need the £1 coin. Ask how the £1 coin differs from the others in colour, shape and thickness. Let the children feel in a bag of mixed coins and pick out the £1 coins without looking.

2 Writing £1 as £1·00

Show the children how we write £1 as £1·00. Explain that the number of pennies is written to the right of the point and that we don't have to write 'p' if we have already written '£'.

Give the children practice in writing the pound sign.

Use plastic coins or drawings on the board to show how we write:

126p as £1·26
104p as £1·04
 68p as £0·68 etc.

Show the children that they must always put two numbers to represent the pence. For example, if 102p is written as £1·2 then it is really 120p or £1·20 that is being written not 102p or £1·02.

A game to play

PLACE THE MONEY

Divide a tray or box into two compartments and clearly label them '£' and 'p'. Write an amount such as £1·15 on the board. Let the children come out and place the correct amount of coins in each section.

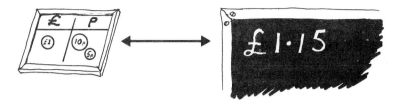

Alternatively, place the money in the tray and ask a child to come out, count it, and write the amount on the board, using the £ sign.

3 Writing bills

If possible, show the children five or six items purchased on the average family's weekly shopping trip and each over £1 in price. Ask a child to choose two items and then write the bill for these and the total cost. Point out that the recording is similar to HTU with the same process of exchange or carrying. A calculator can be used to check the bill.

4 Change

Ask the children to explain why they sometimes get change when shopping.

A game to play

Give some children 20p each. Write out smaller amounts of money on pieces of card and place them face downwards on the table. Each child chooses a card, calls out the amount, goes to the money box, puts the 20p in and takes out the change. Do they understand they are putting in the money they have spent and are taking out the money they have left?

When the children are confident with 20p, the amount can be increased.

5 Subtraction of money

Point out that, like addition of money, subtraction is similar to HTU.

MENTAL WORK   Give the children practice in converting pence to pounds and vice versa.

Give practice in simple addition and subtraction of money. This can extend to verbal problems.

USING THE CALCULATOR

Show the children how to enter amounts of money using the decimal point.

Let them practise changing pence to pounds on the calculator display. For example, call out 136p. Who is first to display 1·36?

Point out that when the calculator shows 1·2 it is really 1·20.

Use the calculator to work out bills and change. For example, 'We have £6·00 and buy two things for £2·46 and £3·27.'

Add 2·46 + 3·27 = 5·73

Clear the display.

6·00 − 5·73 = 0·27, so £0·27 change.

By using the calculator it is possible to work at a level of exchange or carrying that the child has not yet reached.

A classroom shop can give both 'shopkeeper' and 'customer' worthwhile calculator practice.

Children often find it fun to check supermarket bills. They can also help with checking any money collected in school.

LINKS WITH THE ENVIRONMENT

Children will see bills showing pounds and pence when shopping with adults. Look at some long bills from the supermarket checkout. Discuss whether machines always add up correctly and how the cashier must always press the correct buttons.

Talk about buying, paying and receiving change at shops.

When do adults receive bills? For example rates, heating, telephone, clothes, repairs, cleaning, papers, etc.

Children might see large amounts of money being added in school for school trips, tickets for school concerts, school requisition, etc.

NOTES ON INVESTIGATIONS

Section A

Do the children make the investigation easier by placing a £1 coin in the first pot? Do they realise they have to use actual coin values rather than random amounts of money? Do they appreciate that there are many different answers?

Section B

Do the children appreciate that the first column adds up to 13 and therefore one ten is carried to the second column? Do they find different numbers for the second column each time they do the sum?

Section C

Do the children appreciate that the total must be £1·99? Do they use a method? For example, do they first look for three 'units' numbers that add to 9?

Number 15

Purpose

- To revise $\frac{1}{2}$ and $\frac{1}{4}$
- To introduce $\frac{3}{4}$
- To find $\frac{1}{2}$, $\frac{1}{4}$ and $\frac{3}{4}$ of shapes, objects and numbers

Materials

Crayons, squared paper

Vocabulary

Half, quarter, three-quarters, fraction, whole shape, puzzle, squares

TEACHING POINTS

1 Half and quarter

Build up a fraction wall on the board. Ask the children to give the names of the fractions. Talk about how fractions can be equivalent.

1 whole			
$\frac{1}{2}$		$\frac{1}{2}$	
$\frac{1}{4}$	$\frac{1}{4}$	$\frac{1}{4}$	$\frac{1}{4}$

Ask:
'How many halves make one whole?'
'How many quarters are in one whole?'
'How many quarters equals one half?'
Show the children how to write these

$$\frac{2}{2} = 1 \qquad \frac{4}{4} = 1 \qquad \frac{2}{4} = \frac{1}{2}$$

2 Introduce three-quarters

Talk about three-quarters and how to write it as $\frac{3}{4}$.

Ask the children to fold a circle into quarters, colour three of them and label it $\frac{3}{4}$. Can they tell you what fraction is not coloured?

Discuss what the '3' in $\frac{3}{4}$ means.

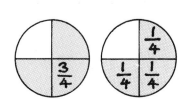

Use strips of paper to make displays.

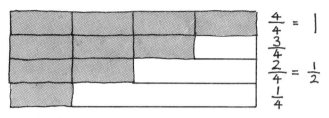

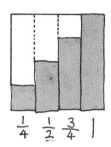

Ask the children to fold squares in various ways to show quarters.

 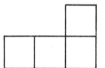  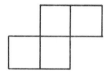

Ask the children to colour $\frac{3}{4}$ of each and talk about the possible ways of doing this.

3 Fractions of numbers

Use squared paper and ask the children to make up different four-square shapes. Ask them to colour $\frac{1}{2}$, $\frac{1}{4}$ or $\frac{3}{4}$ of each of the shapes. Can they tell you what is $\frac{1}{4}$ of 4 squares, $\frac{1}{2}$ of 4 squares and $\frac{3}{4}$ of 4 squares?

Talk with the children about finding $\frac{1}{2}$, $\frac{1}{4}$ and $\frac{3}{4}$ of numbers. To find $\frac{1}{2}$ we divide by 2, to find $\frac{1}{4}$ we divide by 4 and to find $\frac{3}{4}$ we divide by 4 and add 3 of the quarters together.

Give the children a number of objects to draw. Talk about how to find fractions of them.

 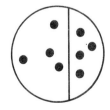

$\frac{1}{2}$ of 6 = 3 $\frac{1}{2}$ of 8 = 4

MENTAL WORK Give practice in finding:
$\frac{1}{2}$ of 2, 4, 6, 8, 10, 12, 14, 16, 18, 20.
$\frac{1}{4}$ of 4, 8, 12.
$\frac{3}{4}$ of 4, 8, 12.

USING THE CALCULATOR Show the children how we can find $\frac{1}{2}$ and $\frac{1}{4}$ of numbers using the calculator by dividing by 2 and 4 respectively. For example, to find $\frac{1}{2}$ of 8 we divide by 2.
Enter $\boxed{8}$ $\boxed{\div}$ $\boxed{2}$ $\boxed{=}$.
NB The numbers must be carefully chosen by the teacher in order to avoid decimals when dividing.

LINKS WITH THE ENVIRONMENT Talk about situations when we might use fractions such as cutting a cake in half, breaking a chocolate bar into quarters, having three-quarters of a pie left. Sometimes, objects such as sweets and marbles are shared into $\frac{1}{2}$s and $\frac{1}{4}$s.
$\frac{1}{2}$s, $\frac{1}{4}$s and $\frac{3}{4}$s are also used in telling the time.

NOTES ON INVESTIGATIONS

Section A

Do the children realise that the whole shape consists of 8 squares? How do they arrive at this conclusion? For example, if two squares is $\frac{1}{4}$ of the shape, how many squares are in the whole shape? Do they draw different whole shapes consisting of 8 squares? Do they see that there are many possibilities in arranging the 8 squares to form a whole one?

Section B

Do the children divide the shape into quarters by drawing horizontal, vertical or diagonal lines? Do they count the squares in order to find what one quarter of 24 is before colouring three quarters? Do the children realise that one quarter of the shape is left uncoloured? Do the children check that the same number of squares have been coloured each time?

Section C

Do the children find it difficult to make up clues when given only the answers? Do they write the fraction or the number first? Do they realise that there are several possibilities for both numbers and fractions?

Length 3

Purpose

- To revise measuring in cm
- To introduce vertical recording of addition of cm, with exchange or carrying
- To introduce subtraction of cm, without exchanging or carrying
- To introduce the metre and 100 cm = 1 m

Materials

Metre ruler, rulers

Vocabulary

Tall, taller, cm, m, metre ruler, wide, long, high, metre, measure, plan, clue, measurement, shape

TEACHING POINTS

1 Addition of centimetres

Talk about when we might need to add cm such as when we need to make things longer. Have the children seen anyone lengthening trousers, dresses, curtains? How was this done?

   Introduce addition of cm to find total length, using practical situations. For example, the skirt is 41 cm long and it is made 5 cm longer. How long is it now?

41 cm

5 cm

41 cm + 5 cm = 46 cm

2 Vertical recording

Show the children how to add cm as they would TU and how they 'carry' or exchange from the units in the same way. Let the children practise one or two additions. Then make up simple problem situations for addition. For example, 'Susan had two pieces of ribbon, 18 cm and 6 cm. What was the total length?' Write a sum to find out.

   Make some strips of paper of different lengths. Let the children pick two each to add up.

   Measure the spans of two children and let the others add them to find the total length. Do the same with shoe lengths and make a display.

15 cm   16 cm   18 cm   15 cm

31 cm   33 cm

3 Difference between

What do we mean by 'difference between'? Show by placing objects side by side or on top of each other.

Have some strips of coloured card of different lengths. Ask two children to choose one each and then lay the shorter one on top of the longer one. Make sure they match at one end. Ask them to measure the difference between the cards.

Ask children to draw and colour strips on squared paper and then to measure the difference.

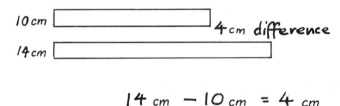

10 cm ⌷_____⌷ 4 cm difference

14 cm ⌷_____⌷

14 cm − 10 cm = 4 cm

4 Take away

Talk about take away situations such as: 'Tom had a piece of string 25 cm long and cut off 14 cm. What was left?' Show the children how to record this and remind them that it is like subtracting TU.

```
      cm
      25
  −   14
      ──
```

Give the children measured strips of paper. Write on the back of each how much they have to cut off. Ask them to work out how much they will have left and then let them actually cut and measure to see if they are right.

5 The metre rule

Show the class or group a metre ruler. Ask how many cm they can see on it, and when they might use it.

Talk about when it is best to measure in cm rather than in m. Can they name things they might measure in metres? Let the children estimate lengths in metres, such as the length of a room, and then ask them to check it by measuring.

They might like to measure a pet at home and make a 'pet passport' giving height, length, etc. or it may be possible to bring a pet into the classroom so that they can all join in the measuring.

Make paper snakes 1 m or 2 m long and link this with work in art.

USING THE CALCULATOR

Explain that addition and subtraction of cm is the same as dealing with T U on the calculator. Let children practise both processes. Give them problems to solve on the calculator such as: 'If I have a stick of rock 26 cm long and I eat 14 cm, how much rock is left?' Talk about how to enter this on the calculator:

LINKS WITH THE ENVIRONMENT

Discuss situations in everyday life where we might add or subtract lengths.

- Lengthening or shortening clothes
- Adding lengths when we are making things, such as two shelves of 42 cm each
- Buying pre-cut lengths of wood from DIY stores and cutting them down to the required length for making rabbit hutches, stilts, goal posts
- Finding out how much taller we are than other people

Discuss the use of metres in everyday life.

- Sports often use metres: for example, the length of swimming baths, 100 m races
- Many household goods are measured in metres, such as material, wire, wallpaper
- Measuring heights of bicycle frames – compare a bike of a seven-year-old with that of an eleven-year-old.
- Comparing heights of family members

NOTES ON INVESTIGATIONS

Section A

Do the children look at the metre rule before they decide what they can buy? Are their choices realistic? Do they think of measuring 5 metres to give them a reference for judging their suggestions? Do they realise that such things as balls of string give them ideal examples?

Section B

Are the children's measurements accurate? Do they use straight lines for easier measuring? If not, how do they measure? Do they design interesting trails? Is each trail 20 cm long?

Section C

Do they begin each clue with the measurement? Do they choose measurements that will help a friend to estimate before actually measuring? Do they give clear clues?

Purpose

- To introduce the kilogram
- To introduce 1 kg = 1000 g and $\frac{1}{2}$ kg = 500 g

Materials

Balance scales, weights (1 kg, 500 g, 200 g, 100 g), plasticine (at least $\frac{1}{2}$ kg per group of children for the Section A investigation), bathroom scales, squared paper, books for the weighing activity, plastic carrier bag, calculator

Vocabulary

Kilogram (kg), gram (g), weigh, weight, balance, heavy, estimate, block graph

TEACHING POINTS

1 The kilogram

Ask the children why we do not weigh only in grams. Can they imagine how many grams an elephant would weigh? Explain that 1000 g = 1 kg and show them the 1 kg weight. Ask them how many grams in half a kilogram. Let them hold a 500 g weight.

2 Estimating kilogram

Show children a 1 kg bag of sugar. Let them hold a 1 kg weight in one hand and the bag of sugar in the other. Ask them if they feel the same.

Ask some children to hold a 1 kg weight and then fill a container with sand until they think it is the same weight. Let them check by weighing. Let them do the same with 500 g. Remind the children to estimate first before checking by weighing.

3 Recording

Talk about how the kilogram is written as kg. Similarly grams are written as g. NB. Plurals do not have an 's': for example, 49 kg, 32 g.

4 Bathroom scales

Show the children some bathroom scales and how to read the kg marks.

Weigh a child of average weight to give children some idea of their own weight. Ask them to estimate the weight of other children and check by using the bathroom scales.

5 Animal weights

Weights of animals appear in the pupils' book, so reference books should be available (see 'Links with the environment').

MENTAL WORK   Give practice in adding up to 1000 g (multiples of 100 g) using classroom gram weights.

LINKS WITH THE ENVIRONMENT   Talk about where we can find, or see, objects marked in grams or kilograms in everyday life. At the grocer's shop or supermarket boxes, tins, packets, potatoes, all have their weight marked in grams or kilograms. Talk about food at home where tins, boxes, jars and packets have their weight shown in grams whilst some weigh exactly 1 kg such as sugar.

Display a set of objects or pictures and let the children sort them into sets of 'less than 1 kg', 'equal to 1 kg' and 'more than 1 kg'.

Children will enjoy comparing the weights of animals from the *Guiness Book of Records*.

Talk about how adults often worry about being overweight or underweight.

NOTES ON INVESTIGATIONS   **Section A**

Because of the amount of plasticine involved it is advisable to let the children work in groups.

Do the children realise how much plasticine is needed and that $\frac{1}{2}$ kg is 500 g? How do they approach the task? Do they weigh the plasticine and then make the animal, or do they make the animal and then weigh it?

Section B

Do the children weigh themselves first in kg on the bathroom scales and use this weight to estimate the others? Are their estimates reasonable? Do they ask if they can check their estimates?

Section C

Do the children weigh an 'average' child (or themselves) and then multiply by the number of children in the class, using a calculator? In the later activity, do they use the weight of the elephant given in the book? Are they able to estimate how many classes are approximately the same weight as an elephant? Are they amazed at their result? (The answer could be about six or more classes.)

Time 3

Purpose

- To introduce minutes for o'clock, half past and quarter past
- To introduce quarter to
- To introduce the digital notation for half past and quarter past

Materials

Clock stamp, stop watch (or one minute timer), newspaper (for TV programmes)

Vocabulary

O'clock, half past, quarter past, quarter to, hand, minutes, hour, earliest, time, order, before, after, longer than

TEACHING POINTS

1 Watches and clocks

Ask the children about the clocks and watches they see. Talk with them about the type of watches they have.

2 Revise o'clock, quarter past, half past

Hold up a demonstration clock face (or a real clock). Set the hands of the clock to an o'clock time and ask what time it is.

Remind the children about the minute and hour hands. Show them how the minute hand moves a quarter of the way around the clock to reach 'quarter past' and half way round to reach 'half past'. Give them practice in telling both of these times.

3 Quarter to

Talk to the children about quarter to times and show the position of the hands.

Talk about fractions of a circle and how we can relate these to the clock face. Explain that when $\frac{3}{4}$ of an hour has gone there is $\frac{1}{4}$ left to go. Two different coloured circles of card slotted together may be used to demonstrate this. (See 'Time 2', page 105.)

Draw clock faces on the board showing quarter to times. Ask the children to state the times.

Make charts showing 'half past', 'quarter past' and 'quarter to' times.

4 Minutes for o'clock, half past, quarter past

Ask the children to sit in silence for one minute. Use a stop watch or one minute timer.

Explain that there are sixty minutes in one hour. Use a clock face to show that half an hour is thirty minutes and a quarter of an hour is fifteen minutes, which may be the length of playtime.

5 Digital notation for half past

Remind the children about the digital recording of o'clock such as 10:00. Talk about which numbers show the hour and which show the minutes. Explain that 10:30 means 10 o'clock and 30 minutes or 'half past 10'.

Draw times on the board using both clock faces and digital notation and talk about them. Ask the children to write or draw them.

Link times on the clock to everyday happenings such as playtime at half past 10.

MENTAL WORK   Give practice in converting digital time to analogue and vice versa.

LINKS WITH THE ENVIRONMENT   Talk about the types of clocks and watches the children see in everyday life.

- On the way to school – clocks in jewellers' shop windows, church clock, town hall clock, bus station clock
- At home – alarm clocks, dining room clock, cooker clock, video clock, watches in the home
- At school – classroom clock, hall clock, stop watches, children's watches

A display of watches and clocks, or pictures of them, can be made.

A topic on early clocks (such as sand clocks, sundials, water clocks) can be linked to other areas of the curriculum such as history, geography, art and craft, science.

NOTES ON INVESTIGATIONS

Section A

Do the children time themselves using a stop watch or sand timer? Do they set themselves realistic targets for activities lasting one minute? At the end of their work do they have an understanding of how long one minute is?

Section B

Do the children easily think up things in school that last fifteen minutes? For example, playtime, time to eat lunch, short assemblies, some school TV programmes, story.

Do they think up activities that take half an hour? For example, PE lessons, music lessons, library time, longer assemblies, netball practice, gym club.

Do they think of things that last about one hour? For example, mathematics lessons, English lessons, games lessons, a school football match, lunchtime.

Section C

You need the TV page of a newspaper for this investigation. Do the children choose the TV programmes which last the correct length of time? Do they choose the children's TV programmes, serials, films? Their choices may lead to discussion of favourite TV programmes and could be linked to work on graphs.

Angles 3

Purpose

- To introduce the right-angle
- To give practice in turning clockwise and anti-clockwise

Materials

Paper, set square (optional), clock face and stamp, squared paper, paper fastener, paper circles, card square

Vocabulary

Quarter turn, right-angle, square corner, set square, clockwise, and anti-clockwise

TEACHING POINTS   ## 1 Right-angles and square corners

Talk with the children about square corners. Do this by rotating geo-strips until they have moved through a quarter turn or a square corner. Explain that another name for a square corner is a right-angle.

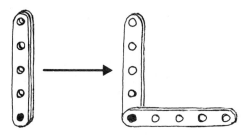

Give children practice in turning through a right-angle and link this with turns to the right and left.

2 Clockwise and anti-clockwise

Talk to the children about clockwise and anti-clockwise turns. Show this by letting the children turn the hands of a working clock clockwise and anti-clockwise.

Put out number cards to show a clock face. Let a child point to 12 and say the order of the numbers as they turn clockwise or anti-clockwise. Ask them if they turned to their right or their left as they went clockwise.

3 More right-angles

Ask a child to face the wall and turn clockwise through a right-angle. What do they then see in front of them?

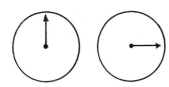

4 More clocks

Talk about clocks again. Tell the children that the minute hand has gone from 12 to 3, and ask what amount of turn it made.

Talk about quarter turns, half turns, and right-angles.

Ask where the hand would be if it turned through two right-angles from 12, or through three right-angles.

5 In the classroom

Ask children to look for right-angles in the classroom: for example, corners of the board, corners of tables, corners of books.

6 Folding right-angles

Let them fold pieces of paper to make right-angles to check square corners.

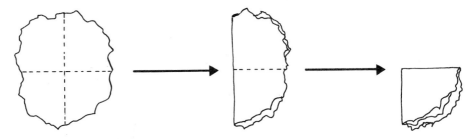

Ask them to look around the classroom and write ten objects that have a right-angle.

7 Right-angles in shapes

Talk about plane shapes such as a square. Ask how many right-angles/square corners it has. Ask them to draw another shape with four right-angles.

Let them draw a triangle with a right-angle.

LINKS WITH THE ENVIRONMENT

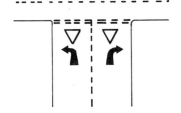

Ask the children to look for right-angles in the environment. For example, we see right-angles in buildings, window frames, doors. Right-angles are also formed where the wall and ceiling meet.

Look for road markings where bicycles or cars must turn through a right-angle.

NOTES ON
INVESTIGATIONS

Section A

Children may find it helpful to have a folded square corner or set square.

Do the children understand that the hands of the clock need to form a square corner? Do they find the 3 o'clock and 9 o'clock position?

NB. Some children may go on to give such times as quarter past 6. This gives the opportunity to discuss, if wished, the fact that the time would have to be 'just past' because of the small movement of the hour hand. It is not anticipated at this point in the scheme that children would be asked to state an exact number of minutes.

Section B

Do the children draw closed shapes? Do they draw in the number of right-angles first before 'closing' the shapes? Do they mark in all the right-angles?

Here are some possible answers.

 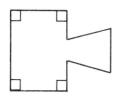 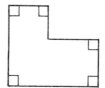 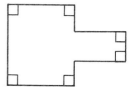

Section C

It is useful for this investigation if children have a 'dial' made from a circle of card, a piece of card and a paper fastener.

Do the children understand that once a number appears at the top of the dial, it becomes the starting point of the next move? Do the children give clear instructions? Do they begin by stating which was the starting number at the top? (It need not, of course, be 1.) Do they then state both the amount and direction of the turns they make?

Module 4 Pupils' book 1
RECORD SHEET

Class . . . .   Pupil . . . .

Topic	Section	Assessment	Comment
Number 1	A B C		
Number 2	A B C		
Shape 1	A B C		
Number 3	A B C		
Area 1	A B C		
Number 4	A B C		
Data 1	A B C		
Money 1	A B C		
Number 5	A B C		
Length 1	A B C		
Weight 1	A B C		
Volume and capacity 1	A B C		
Time 1	A B C		
Angles 1	A B C		
Number 6	A B C		
Number 7	A B C		
Shape 2	A B C		
Number 8	A B C		
Area 2	A B C		

General comments:

Module 4 Pupils' book 2
RECORD SHEET

Class . . . .   Pupil . . . .

Topic	Section	Assessment	Comment
Number 9	A B C		
Data 2	A B C		
Money 2	A B C		
Number 10	A B C		
Length 2	A B C		
Weight 2	A B C		
Volume and capacity 2	A B C		
Time 2	A B C		
Angles 2	A B C		
Number 11	A B C		
Number 12	A B C		
Shape 3	A B C		
Number 13	A B C		
Area 3	A B C		
Number 14	A B C		
Data 3	A B C		
Money 3	A B C		
Number 15	A B C		
Length 3	A B C		
Weight 3	A B C		
Time 3	A B C		
Angles 3	A B C		

General comments:

MATERIALS REQUIRED FOR MODULE 4 ▬▬▬

abacus
bags (small plastic)
balance scales
bathroom scales
beakers
books
bottle
bowl
boxes (different sized
    pairs of red and
    yellow)
bucket
calculators
card
chalk box
circles
clock faces
clock stamp
coins
containers (a selection
    of grocery
    containers,
    some one litre,
    some more than one
    litre, and some less)
cotton reels
counters
crayons
cubes
cup
egg cup
elastic bands
equilateral triangles
feather
funnel
glue

a copy of the Highway
    Code
jug
kettle
plastic knives
labels
1 litre measure
$\frac{1}{2}$ litre measure
macaroni
marbles
margarine tubs
metre rule
mug
multiplication squares
newspaper
number cards
number lines
100 board
100 squares
paint pot
paper (plain)
paper plates
paper strips
paper fasteners
peas (dried)
pencils
pens (felt tipped)
place-value boards
plastic bottle
plastic carrier bag
plasticine (at least $\frac{1}{2}$ kg
    per group of
    children)
plasticine boards
rectangles
rulers

scissors
set square (optional)
shoe
solid shapes (square-
    based pyramid,
    triangular prism,
    cube, cuboid,
    cylinder, cone,
    sphere)
spike abacus
spoon (wooden)
spotty paper
squared paper
stone
stop watch or sand
    timer
straws
string
structural apparatus
tape measure
teapot
teaspoon
templates (circles,
    squares, equilateral
    triangles, hexagons,
    pentagons,
    octagons, rectangle)
tin
tracing paper
watch
water
weights (1 kg, 500 g,
    200 g, 100 g, 50 g,
    20 g, 10 g, 5 g)
yogurt pots

GLOSSARY FOR MODULE 4

abacus	An abacus is a piece of apparatus used for counting/displaying numbers. For example

spike abacus

counting frame

algorithm	An algorithm is a method or a procedure for finding a solution. For example, decomposition is an algorithm for subtraction.
angle	An angle is the amount of turn or rotation. Angles are measured in degrees with 360° in a whole turn.
anti-clockwise	*See* clockwise.
apparatus	Apparatus is equipment, for example, ruler, counters.
arbitrary units	Arbitrary units are non-standard units, for example, spans, cubits.
area	Area is the size or amount of a surface, and is usually written in units of square measurement.
axis (*plural* **axes**)	Axes are the number lines drawn on a graph. These number lines are usually horizontal and vertical.
balance	A balance is a set of scales.
barter	To barter means to give one thing in exchange for another.
bilateral symmetry	*See* symmetry.
block graph	A block graph is a form of pictorial representation where the data is represented by columns.
circle	A circle is a set of points, all of which are a fixed distance (the radius) from a fixed point (the centre).

radius

circle

clockwise	This is the direction in which the hands of a clock turn. Anti-clockwise is the opposite direction.
column	A column is a list of numbers (or letters) or squares in a grid going down a page.
commutative	An operation for example, $(+, -)$ is commutative if numbers can be used with it in any order and still give the same answer. Addition is commutative, since, for example, $3 + 1 = 1 + 3$. Multiplication is commutative, since, for example, $3 \times 2 = 2 \times 3$. Subtraction is **not** commutative, since $3 - 1 \neq 1 - 3$. Division is **not** commutative, since $4 \div 2 \neq 2 \div 4$.
cone	A cone is a solid which has a circular base and tapers to a point at the top.

constant function   The use of the constant function on a calculator allows numbers to increase or decrease by a fixed amount. For example, the numbers 2, 5, 8, 11, . . . can be given by the constant + 3.

corner   A corner is a point where two lines meet. It may also be called a vertex. For example, a triangle has three corners or vertices. In this course, 'corner' is used for plane shapes and 'vertex' for solid shapes.

cube   A cube is a solid with all its six faces square and all its edges equal in length. For example, a die is a cube.

cubit   A cubit is the distance from the elbow to the tip of the outstretched longest finger.

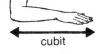
cubit

cuboid   A cuboid is a solid with six faces that are all rectangles. Opposite faces are the same.

cylinder   A cylinder is a solid with the shape of a circle along its length.

data   Data is information or facts which have been collected. It is often displayed as a block graph, or pie chart.

decomposition   Decomposition is a method for subtraction where, for example, a 'ten' is changed into ten units.

$$\begin{array}{r} 5^12^14 \\ -\ 3\ 1\ 7 \\ \hline 2\ 0\ 7 \end{array}$$

digit   A digit is a single figure or symbol in a number system. For example, the digits in 347 are 3, 4 and 7.

digital clock   A digital clock is a clock which shows the time in number form, for example 11:23

edge   An edge is the line formed when two faces of a solid meet.

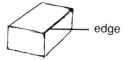
edge

equilateral triangle   An equilateral triangle is a triangle with all three sides the same length.

equivalent fractions   Fractions are equivalent if they can represent the same fraction. For example, $\frac{1}{2}, \frac{2}{4}, \frac{3}{6}, \frac{4}{8}, \frac{5}{10}, \frac{6}{12}$ are all equivalent.

estimate   To estimate is to make an approximate judgement of a number, amount, etc. without measuring it.

face   A face is the flat side of a solid shape.

factor   A factor is a number which divides exactly into another number. For example, 3 is a factor of 12.

gram   A gram is a unit of mass. It is $\frac{1}{1000}$ of a kilogram. The abbreviation for gram is g.

graph	A graph is a picture or diagram to make information more easily understood. Data is often shown by picture graphs, block graphs or pie charts.
hexagon	A hexagon is a plane shape with six sides. A regular hexagon has all its sides equal in length and all its angles the same size.
kilogram	A kilogram is the standard unit of mass (abbreviation: kg). A kilogram is equal to 1000 grams.
line of symmetry	A line of symmetry on a shape divides the shape into halves so that one half is a mirror image of the other.
litre	A litre is a unit of capacity (abbreviation: l, not to be confused with 1). One litre is a little over $1\frac{3}{4}$ pints.
magic square	A magic square has numbers on a square grid such that each row, column and diagonal add up to the same total. This is a 3×3 magic square.

2	7	6
9	5	1
4	3	8

mass	The mass of an object is the amount of matter in it. It is linked to weight but is not exactly the same. The weight of an object is determined by the force of gravity acting upon it.
measure	To measure is to find a size or quantity by comparison with a fixed unit.
metre	A metre is the standard unit of length (abbreviation: m).
multiple	Multiples of a number are given by that number multiplied by whole numbers. The multiples of 4 are 4, 8, 12, 16, . . . The multiples of 10 are 10, 20, 30, 40, . . .
multiplication square	A multiplication square is a square which shows the multiplication table.

×	1	2	3
1	1	2	3
2	2	4	6
3	3	6	9

number bond	A number bond is a relationship between a set of numbers. The following are examples of number bonds: $3 + 4 = 7$, $9 - 1 = 8$, $2 \times 5 = 10$, $12 \div 2 = 6$.
number line	A number line is a line with a set of points which correspond to numbers, for example,

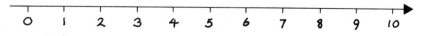

number sentence	A number sentence is a mathematical statement or sentence, for example, $2 + 1 = 3$.
octagon	An octagon is an eight-sided plane shape. A regular octagon has all its sides equal in length and all its angles the same size.

pattern	A pattern is an arrangement of numbers, etc. according to a rule. A pattern allows us to predict what might come next. For example, in the sequence 1, 2, 3, −, −, 6, the missing numbers are 4, 5, since the pattern is adding one each time.
pentagon	A pentagon is a five-sided plane shape. A regular pentagon has all its sides equal in length and all its angles the same size.
picture graph	A picture graph or pictogram is a way of representing information using pictures or drawings.
place value	Place value is the value of a symbol or digit in a number system due to its position. For example, in the number 22, each 2 has a different value because of its position.
plane shape	A plane shape is a two-dimensional shape. For example, circles and triangles are plane shapes.
polygon	A polygon is a many-sided plane shape. A triangle is a three-sided polygon.
prism	A prism is a solid with the same shape along its length, so that it has uniform cross-sections. This is a triangular prism.

pyramid	A pyramid is a solid shape with a polygon for its base. The other faces are triangles which meet at a vertex called the apex.

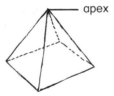

apex

reach	A person's reach is the length from finger tip to finger tip when the arms are extended sideways.

reach

rectangle	A rectangle is a four-sided shape with four right-angles and opposite sides equal in length.
regular shape	A regular shape has all its sides the same length and all its angles the same size, for example, a square.
right-angle	A right-angle is a quarter of a complete turn. It is measured as an angle of 90°.
row	A row is a list of numbers or letters across the page.
set square	A set square is an instrument for finding right-angles.
shopkeeper's addition	Shopkeeper's addition is a method of doing subtraction by using addition or counting on. Suppose a child buys a toy for 14p and gives the shopkeeper a 20p coin. The shopkeeper gives the change by counting on from 14p until 20p is reached: 14p + 1p + 5p = 20p.
solid	A solid is a three-dimensional shape, for example, a cube.

span	A span is the distance across a hand from the outstretched little finger to the thumb.

sphere	A sphere is the mathematical name for a round ball.
spiral	A spiral is a curve which winds around a fixed point and moves away from it.

fixed point

square	A square has four equal sides and four right-angles
square corner	A square corner is a right-angle.
standard unit	Standard units are generally accepted units. A standard unit for measuring length is the metre. A standard unit for measuring weight is the kilogram.
stride	A stride is a long step measured by the distance from heel to heel or toe to toe.

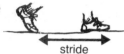
stride

structural apparatus	Structural apparatus is apparatus to show how the number system works.
symmetry	Line symmetry is the exact matching of parts on either side of a straight line. This is sometimes called bilateral or mirror symmetry.
tally	A tally is a method of recording data by drawing a line for each item counted. For example, 8 cars might be recorded as ‖‖ ‖‖ ‖‖ → 8.
template	A template is an object or shape to draw around.
total	A total is the whole amount or the sum.
triangle	A triangle is a plane shape with three straight sides.

 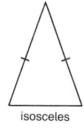  

equilateral   isosceles   right-angled   scalene

triangular prism	A triangular prism is a prism whose end faces are triangles.
vertex (*plural* **vertices**)	The vertex is a point where lines or edges meet.

vertex

vertices	*See* vertex.
volume	The volume of a solid is the amount of space it occupies. The units of measurement are usually cubic centimetres or cubic metres.
weight	The weight of an object depends on the gravitational force acting on it. An object on the Moon will weigh less than on Earth although its mass will remain the same.